Twentieth-Century Houses

EUROPE

Twentieth-Century Houses

Olivier Boissière

Europe

TERRAIL

Cover page

House in London
Future Systems, 1994.

Preceding page

Casa Malaparte, Capri, 1942.

English Translation: Malcolm Imrie
Editorial Director: Jean-Claude Dubost
Editorial Assistants: Geneviève Meunier, Hélène Roquejoffre and Claire Néollier
Editorial Aide: Chris Miller and Hélène Cœur
Cover Design: Laurent Gudin
Art Director: Bruno Leprince
Typesetting and Filmsetting: DV Arts Graphiques, Chartres
Photoengraving: Litho Service T. Zamboni, Verona

© FINEST SA / PIERRE TERRAIL EDITIONS, PARIS 1998
The Art Book Subsidiary of BAYARD PRESSE SA
English edition: © october 1998
Publisher's n°: 217
ISBN 2-87939-185-7
Printed in Italy

Contents

Teaching staff on the roof
of the workshop block
of the Dessau Bauhaus in 1925.
From left to right: Josef Albers,
Hinnerk Scheper, Georg Muche,
Lazlo Moholy-Nagy, Herbert Bayer,
Joost Schmid, Walter Gropius,
Marcel Breuer, Wassili Kandinsky,
Paul Klee, Lyonel Feininger, Gunta
Sharon-Stölzl, Oskar Schlemmer.

Introduction

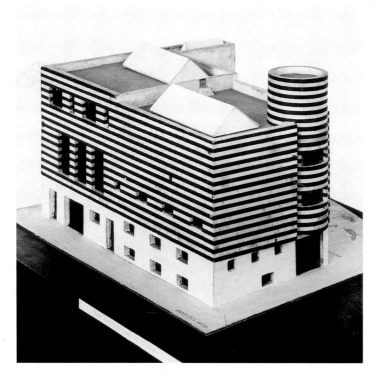

Adolf Loos:
Plan for a house
for Joséphine Baker 1926.

Our century is drawing to a close. It has brought with it every possible hope, and every possible disillusion. From spectacular progress to bloody conflicts, history has deployed its full arsenal of dreams and nightmares. Humanity, that sorcerer's apprentice, has remained a powerless witness to the daunting acceleration of which it is also the instrument. In the exodus from the countryside, the demographic explosion, and the rise in life expectancy, human settlements have experienced the successive shocks of an era of unprecedented growth. We have built more during this century than in the entire history of humanity. It might be thought that architecture would necessarily draw some advantage from this. But such has not been the case. Architecture is the expression of a civilisation, the reflection of a society, contradictory, fragmented and even, at times, democratic. It is forced to undergo social mutations it can neither anticipate nor (through a political role) determine. Dependent on economics, on technological and cultural change and even, in recent times, on the vagaries of fashion, architecture can never be more than the belated product of its epoch. It is the privilege of architecture to be a public art. But it is also dependent, and therefore slow. That is its original weakness. Architects of this century have done everything in their power to remedy it; they have attended to social movements, allied themselves to artistic avant-gardes, and tracked the progress of science and technology. They have even attempted to anticipate demand, thus exposing themselves to outrage, incomprehension, and ridicule. In Marseilles, where he built his famous *Unité d'Habitation*, Le Corbusier was long known as the *fada* (screwball). Architecture needs to be accepted, if not acceptable. It is a reasonable art. As one major contemporary practitioner used to say, you shouldn't push your client over the cliff.

The house, the *domus*, the home, is at once refuge and shelter. It is the place of communion for the nuclear family and its social representation, the primary cell in which one eats, drinks, and sleeps, copulates or watches television, washes, urinates and defecates, meditates and reads, dreams and sometimes works. It is both a public and very private place. The delights of cities and social promiscuity are real, but everyone dreams of having a home. For architects, it poses a thorny but irresistible challenge, giving rise to a whole range of complex little problems. Could any architect turn down the opportunity to build a house? On the other hand, does any other architectural genre so expose one's talents and weaknesses? For such small returns? Is the game really worth the candle? The architect, designing a house, is naked and defenceless.

There is something a little contradictory in all the well-established ideas about domestic architecture. For some, it offers the utmost freedom to architects, who can test their new (and revolutionary) ideas, investing in the house all their hitherto repressed fantasies. For others, it is the *locus* where mutual confidence must be attained, or separate outlooks – those of architect and occupier-user-client – confronted. And to whom will the realised project belong? "The Villa Laroche" is also called, interchangeably, "the Corbusier House" in the Rue du Docteur-Blanche.

Taking the three fundamental principles proclaimed by Vitruvius – solidity, utility and beauty – it may be that the client and the architect can agree straight away on the first, which largely depends on good sense and the current state of technology. But as soon as it becomes a question of utility, one enters the private sphere. The architect is, by vocation, the intruder here. What of the client's bathroom or bedroom habits? The relationship becomes indiscreet. The confessions it requires border on the psychoanalytic and relate to the habits of passion. Still, these are problems that can be settled without discomfiture.

Beauty is the hard nut to crack. True, clients choose an architect on the basis of what they assume to be a degree of aesthetic community. But tastes and colours are a matter for discussion; or would be, if the architect were not convinced that, in this field, he alone is the legitimate authority. He may bow to others' judgement when it comes to the solidity of the building or the positioning of a wash-basin. But beauty is *his* concern. All the more so because, in the last analysis, that is what he's paid for. Here lies the overweening ambiguity of the client-architect couple: it is a relationship of reciprocal trust, complicity, even affection. But it is also an *interested* relationship, with all the concomitant baggage of suspicion. In histories of architecture, a happy ending is the exception that proves the rule.

The partnership of architect and client is an ephemeral one. Historians of modern architecture have tended to overlook the client in their praise of the architect, no doubt sparing his blushes in the process. This is, of course, unfair. It takes two to tango, as one American actor and president aptly put it. History is there to show us that there is no great architecture without great patrons.

History is properly invoked here. A good number of the dwellings presented in this book already belong to history, whether by being listed, protected or simply recognised. Some are comfortably lived in, others converted to new uses: they are managed, administered, worked on, and this is all to the good. Others still, placed under the protection of public or private institutions, are devoutly visited by a cultured public. Embalmed in their original state or emptied of their fixtures and fittings, they have become monuments. Monuments posing questions both profound and boorish. For their legitimacy is equivocal. Gertrude Stein once noted that a museum cannot be modern and a museum. And neither Aloysus Riegl, who pioneered the notion of heritage, nor Françoise Choay, who addressed only the issues of the historical past, throw much light on the problem. Are these monuments valuable because they are old? They are the symbols of our modernity. Should we, then, value them for being new? They belong to other times, to outdated technologies and outmoded aesthetics. Is it their artistic value, then, their *Kunstwollen*, that makes them cult objects? But a house is a living organism which cannot do without a woman's perfume, a telephone ringing in the distance or the smell of a pot-au-feu on the stove... And we have scarcely resolved this puzzle before the Byzantine quarrels between conservationists grow strident. Here is a house that has been leaking since the twenties. Is it proper to repair it with a Neoprene seal? Such uncertainties!

That these dwellings – witnesses to the modernity of our century (in our cautious definition) – are of the utmost fascination, one may easily grasp. It is clear that they still speak directly to the man in the street. They tell us that the spirit of the times is as certain as it is fantastical. They tell us architecture is still unknown. They tell us that our century was indeed worth living in.

Hector Guimard:
entrance
to Castel Béranger
1897-1898

The Pioneers

Art Nouveau, Modern Style, Jugendstil, Secession, *nouille*, *métro*, *modernisme*–what everyone agreed was a new *style* spread across the whole of Europe in a few short years. Its birthplace was not the great metropolises, but cities generally considered–not without condescension–to be provincial: Brussels, Glasgow, Turin, Vienna in its fading glory. From these it spread to Paris, then throughout Europe, as far as its northern frontiers where it merged with national forms of romanticism. Today, the mysteries of its origins are an open secret: the writings of Ruskin and Morris, the English Arts and Crafts movement, and above all the *fin-de-siècle* aesthetic that celebrated nature, flowers and women, those evanescent subjects of symbolist and Pre-Raphaelite painting. We know, too, that it represented a kind of last stand, a doomed resistance to the irresistible rise of industry and standardisation, a desperate attempt to roll back the encroaching tide of urbanisation, an anticipated nostalgia for an unspoilt, natural world that every new day diminishes.

The overwhelming success of Art Nouveau was very short-lived. After Cubism, the Great War and the proletarian revolution, Proust's *jeunes filles en fleurs* survived only on the beach at Cabourg and in the gardens of the Champs-Élysées. Art Nouveau was not spared by history. It was a style belonging to the Belle Epoque and thus a futile one; a pleasant diversion for aesthetes, those accomplices of a bourgeoisie enlightened but unashamedly paternalistic. Only later was it perceived that, beneath its light and bucolic surfaces, there lay a genuinely innovative force. For in their rationalisation of construction in metal, their scorn for the laws of composition, their timid opening up of the plan to greater spatial freedom, the architects of Art Nouveau were, in their own way, preparing the revolution. And Gaudí, the freest, most audacious and lunatic among them, was inventing an organic and figurative architecture whose eternal recurrence has been celebrated throughout the 20th century.

Hôtel Solvay

Brussels, Belgium, 1894-1900

Victor Horta

Left
Behind the opulent exterior of a turn-of-the-century, aristocratic town-house, the Hôtel Solvay contains many highly innovative features: reversal of the traditional town-house plan, use of metal in domestic architecture, opening up of space, and an original ornamental aesthetic.

Following pages
The grand entrance with finely-worked marble floor, illuminated by lamps on metal pillars with petal-shaped shades. The painting by Théo Van Rysselberghe gives a foretaste of the play of light on the first floor.

Even before the turn of the century, Victor Horta had shown himself to be a great reformer. He was the first strictly to apply the principles of modern architecture as set out by Viollet-le-Duc. The latter had proclaimed the rationalist character of construction, its logic and truth. He had asserted its subordination to programme, defined the façade as expression of the internal layout of a building. He conceived a building as a harmony of elements – furniture, ironwork, woodwork, fabrics – in short, as an all-encompassing design. In a few short years, Horta vindicated this approach. He did so in buildings mostly commissioned by progressive Brussels society: houses for the engineer Tassel and the industrialist Van Eetvelde, the *Maison du Peuple* for the Brussels federation of the Belgian Worker's Party, and the department store *L'Innovation*. But his greatest achievement is no doubt the Hôtel Solvay.

Armand Solvay was a cosmopolitan industrialist, an enlightened

patron and a philanthropist. When the two men met, the architect, who already had a number of remarkable buildings to his credit, was barely thirty-one years old. Solvay, who had just married Fanny Hunter, was twenty-nine. Together, they built a masterpiece of Art Nouveau.

The site was long and narrow, and the façade on the Avenue Louise was a modest one. Horta's first innovation was to rotate the traditional plan of a Parisian hôtel by ninety degrees, placing the main entrance beside the wall of the adjoining building in the terrace. Carriages would pass through the gateway, deposit their occupants and continue to the stables at the back of the garden. A vestibule flanked by a smoking-room and an enormous kitchen opening on to the garden occupied the ground floor. From there, the main staircase rose to the first floor, its single flight dividing in two at the first landing to form a monumental reception area. Here Horta introduced another crucial innovation: he minimised the use of stone and brick, in favour of extensive ironwork, and opened up a vast central light-well which establishes the airy character of the building. He also created lateral perspectives between the façades and flooded all the reception rooms with natural light.

This *mise en scène,* together with the calculated harmony of the height and breadth of the stairs, was explicitly intended to "prioritise breathing-space" as Yolande Oostens Wittamer has stressed in her study of the hôtel. We should note, too, the innovative and efficient means of circulating warm air, which ensured equal temperatures throughout the building. Beyond such purely technical matters, Horta took pains discreetly to govern the movement of bodies in space, and to favour physical well-being and calm. Light, movement and ventilation, no less than the originality of the aesthetic, were intended to stimulate spiritual activity. The furniture, all designed by Horta, the coloured motifs, the panelling in precious woods, the marble and the serpentine ironwork, formed a perfect environment for the spiritual life of the turn-of-the-century gentleman.

When Louis Wittamer acquired the town-house in 1958, it had already suffered the ravages of time and war: a shell had destroyed the vast glass canopy over the grand staircase. Art Nouveau had fallen out of favour, and the new owner's friends mocked him for his purchase. But Louis Wittamer was aware of the responsibility history had bestowed on him. After patient and scrupulous research, the house will gradually be restored to something very close to its original state, and the glass roof will be carefully reconstructed. Today the Hôtel Solvay offers visitors the magnificent and colourful spectacle of a grand residence from the dawn of the 20th century.

The sinuous façade with its wrought-iron balconies has retained certain classic characteristics: symmetry of composition and tripartite division into base, body and crowning.

Left
The suite of drawing rooms, barely separated by doors that are largely glass-panelled, displays all the refinement of woodwork and furniture designed by the master.

Villa Majorelle, or Villa Jika

Nancy, France, 1898-1900

Henri Sauvage

Crowned by a pointed roof and picturesque chimneys, the west façade of the house has a projecting and slightly incongruous balcony, attesting to the young Henri Sauvage's freedom of expression.

By 1897, Louis Majorelle, artist and cabinet-maker, had turned his family business into one of the leading concerns of the Nancy school. His furniture, lamps, ironworks, and interior designs inspired by nature had gradually acquired a most flattering reputation. This was the moment he chose to set up new premises in which to rationalise his production. The large site that he purchased lay on the edge of the old town and commanded fine views of the neighbouring hills. Weissenburger, who became a prominent architect in the Nancy school, built him gleaming new workshops. Then in 1898, a young man rebelling against the teaching of the École des Beaux-Arts, the son-in-law of the sculptor Alexandre Charpentier, an old friend of Majorelle, invited Majorelle to create the furniture and interior designs for the Café de Paris in the Avenue de l'Opéra.

Henri Sauvage was twenty-five. He had no qualifications, but had already demonstrated his talents. When Majorelle decided to

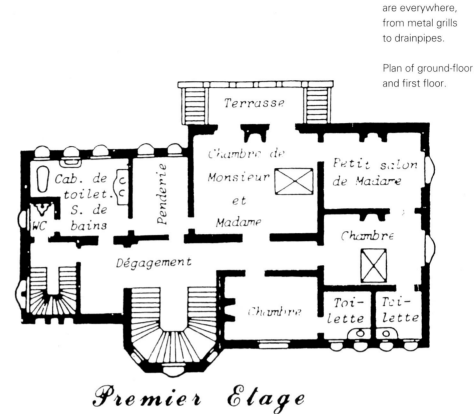

Premier Etage

The overhanging
balcony of Louis
Majorelle's studio.

A flight of steps
bordered with
zoomorphic shapes,
created by
the ceramicist
Alexandre Bigot,
leads to the terrace.

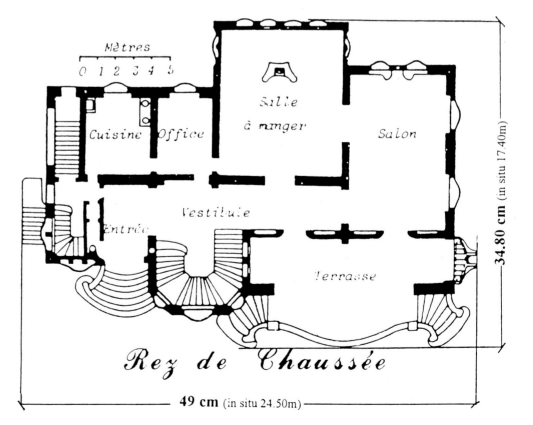

Rez de Chaussée

34.80 cm (in situ 17.40m)

49 cm (in situ 24.50m)

The contorted profile
of the carved banisters,
designed by
Henri Sauvage.

Previous pages
The dining room
is full of furniture
by Majorelle, who used
the house to exhibit
his work. Right
in the middle
of the room,
the sculptural fireplace
by Alexandre Bigot,
with its flame and
melting lava motif.

Right
The fireplace
in the drawing room
is crowned
by a multicoloured
stained-glass work
by Jacques Gruber.

build his villa, it was to this neophyte that he confided the task. Before slamming the door of the École des Beaux-Arts, Sauvage had been a frequent visitor to the studio of Pascal, a disciple of Labrouste. He was a confirmed rationalist who had acquired a passion for Art Nouveau through contact with Majorelle and the Nancy school. The Villa Jika (its name derives from the initials of Majorelle's wife) bears the traces of this double affiliation. Its overall design is strictly functional, answering to the needs of a bourgeois home, slightly modified by the need to provide a showroom for the owner's work. On the ground-floor were the reception rooms and adjoining services, on the first floor the master bedrooms, and under the roof the servants' quarters, along with a huge studio where Majorelle practised sculpture. Aside from its decoration, which is very much of its period, the originality of the building undoubtedly lies in Sauvage's wish to provide for the functional requirements of each element before uniting them into a single construction. The result is a series of different spaces collocated on functional principles with blithe candour. The dining room juts out from the south face to support a balcony on the master bedroom, high saddleback roofs crown the studio, and the staircase lends a jagged outline to the north façade. The belvedere from which Majorelle could contemplate the sunset was conceived and built as an incongruous addition. When we note the 6-4-2 window plan of the service façade, we perceive a whole whose very imperfection jubilantly proclaims its freedom and thumbs its nose at conformity.

This joyful freedom is also found in the decoration, for which Majorelle and Sauvage joined forces with the ceramist Bigot and the stained-glass maker Gruber. Objects and decors bear witness to their imagination and their skill. A few examples: the monumental fireplace in the centre of the dining room whose chimney flue in lava-stone echoes the flames of the hearth; the entrance with its overhanging porch of glass and wrought iron, its front door decorated with an honesty-flower motif repeated in the coatrack and reflected in the mirror at the back to give the effect of depth of field behind the viewer; and the staircase with its ivy motif, dimly lit by Gruber's stained glass. There is an almost frivolous exuberance in the villa Majorelle which extends to fine technical details, like the gutters and drainpipes with floral motifs.

Thanks to his friend Francis Jourdain, the young Sauvage would find other opportunities to express himself in the Art Nouveau idiom, in particular on the occasion of the 1900 World Exhibition in Paris, where he was commissioned to design the Guignol and Loïe Fuller pavilions (only, perhaps, in Belle Epoque, could dancers be celebrated alongside the benefactors of humanity!). A free spirit, he moved on to other fields without a backward glance: in 1912 he developed a form of workers' housing, built in progressively stepped-back terraces, and constructed his masterpiece, the 'maisons ouvrières' in the Rue Vavin in Paris, which have earned him a place in the history of 20th century architecture.

Hill House

Helensburgh, Scotland, 1903-1904

Charles Rennie Mackintosh

A country outing with
the 'Immortals' assembled
around Mackintosh. At the
rear, Frances Macdonald;
from left to right, Margaret
Macdonald, wife of
Mackintosh, Katherine
Cameron, Janet Aitken, Agnes
Raeburn, Jessie Keppie and
unidentified bearded man;
in the foreground,
Herbert MacNair and
Charles Rennie Mackintosh.

Left
The hall of Hill House:
Mackintosh's geometric
style can be seen
in the austere right angles
and perpendiculars and
the repeated squares, allied
here with a subtle range
of colours and a discreet
Japanese influence.

When Mackintosh first began work on the proposed Hill House for the publisher Walter Blackie in 1903, he was only thirty-five. But by that time the most important part of his architectural work was already behind him. He was a highly precocious architect, gaining attention during his studies at the Glasgow School of Art for his talents as a painter and designer. He won a scholarship which allowed him to travel in France and Italy in 1890-1891, subsequently designing a new building for the Glasgow School of Art, his masterpiece, at twenty-eight. By the time he met Blackie he had completed the first phase of this building, and had also created numerous interiors and furniture designs, a house at Windy Hill, Kilmacolm, and a chain of tea-rooms for the famous Mrs Cranston. He gained an international reputation with exhibitions of his work in Turin, Darmstadt and, especially, Vienna, where his influence on Josef Hoffmann and Koloman, also known as Kolo (Karl) Moser, was considerable. By 1903, Mackintosh was an experienced architect with a mature talent. His rigorous approach, the austerity of his interior designs, and his taste for abstraction earned him Mies van der Rohe's tribute: 'purifier of

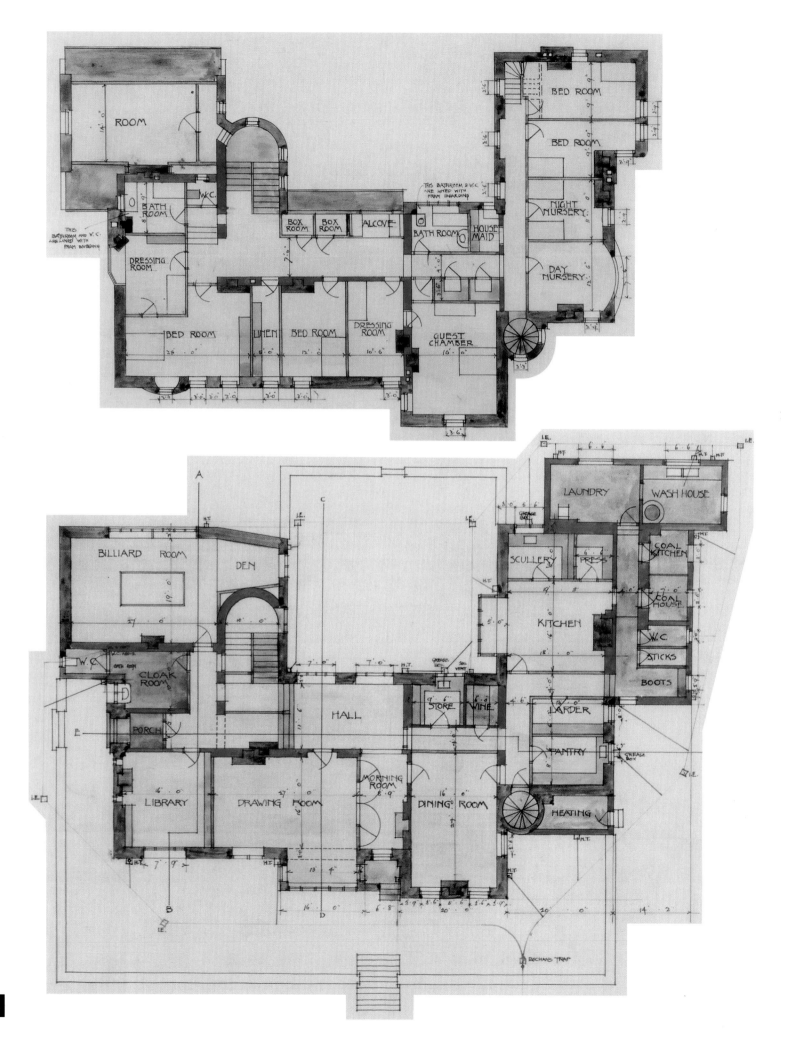

Left
Original floor-plans.
Blackie crossed
out the billiard-room
and the corresponding
room on the first floor.

Views of the house
and grounds:
the volumes directly
reflect the internal
layout, in complete
defiance of the classical
laws of composition.

architecture'. He also called him a 'shooting star'. For by the start of the Great War, new commissions were rare. No doubt this was partly explained by the times, but it was also because, behind the seductive charm, there was a touchy, difficult man. He took himself off to London, then to Port-Vendres, where he led a modest and retiring life. He died in 1928, well before his place in architectural history was acknowledged.

Walter Blackie was a prosperous publisher, and a man of culture, open to the new ideas of his time. His art director, Talwyn Morris, was a brilliant adept of the 'Glasgow' decorative style, developed in the 1890s by 'The Four' (Herbert MacNair, the MacDonald sisters and Mackintosh himself). It was Morris who advised Blackie to engage Mackintosh for his new house. Blackie owned a piece of land at the top of a hill overlooking the little town of Helensburgh. The landscape was harsh and beautiful: a violent, variable climate, constantly changing light, bare, red moorland, clouds jetting across the sky, and the grey waters of the Clyde estuary whipped up by squalls. Mackintosh had built the Windy Hill house on a similar site at Kilmacolm. Blackie visited it. The two men got on from the start: both disapproved of the kind of eclectic pastiche that was in fashion at the time and appreciated the awkwardly functional elegance of vernacular building. Relations were helped by Mackintosh's rare capacity to listen to and respect the wishes of his clients. Blackie placed his full confidence in him. This did not stop him from eliminating at a stroke of the pen the planned billiard room in the north-west wing: he didn't play billiards.

The main part of the house had a perfectly functional configuration matching the Blackies' life style: the spheres of professional and family life were carefully separated. Blackie received his visitors and clients in a library-office right beside the entrance, at the beginning of a long hallway giving on to the drawing room and dining room. Further on was the service wing. Above, the bedrooms were arranged to make the most of the southern orientation, allowing them to enjoy the panorama of the estuary visible beyond the gates and walls of the garden.

Hill House is one of the most perfect examples of Mackintosh's integral design. Details and ensemble are wholly at one: austere furniture, tall, straight-backed chairs, the dominant pattern of squares and trellises, repeated floral motifs forming almost abstract friezes, and vertical lines picked out in silver. Of particular virtuosity are the drawing room and its extension into the window space, with its fireplaces encrusted with mother-of-pearl; and Mrs Blackie's bedroom, with its vaulted alcove echoing the decorative oval motifs. The bedroom bore witness to the marital conventions of the time: Walter Blackie had a little adjoining room with a camp-bed and a view over the estuary. From this window, legend has it, he watched the departure of ships laden with his books and awaited their return laden with his money.

Left
The fireplace in the drawing room crowned by a painting by Margaret Macdonald. The mother-of-pearl and lilac motifs are found on walls and furniture alike.

Mackintosh's wife's bedroom: note the rose motifs on the walls and the geometrically patterned furniture.

Details of decoration on the fireplace and chest of drawers.

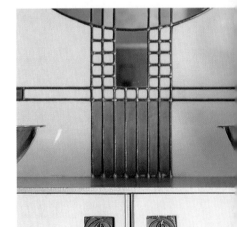

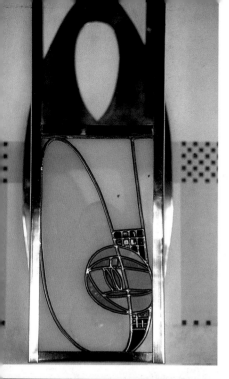

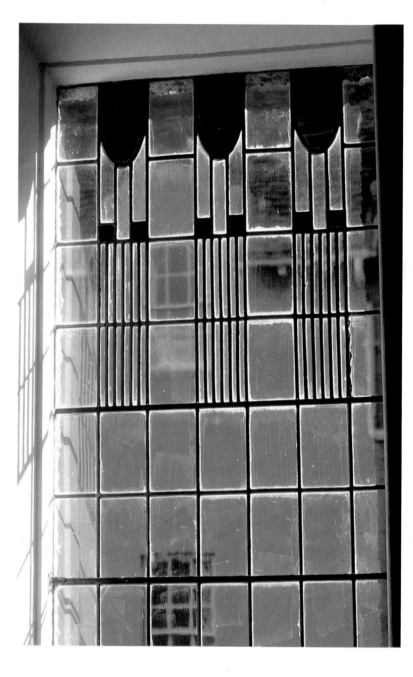

The austere geometry gives way to pearl- and lilac-shaded motifs in the family rooms, but returns in Blackie's office-library (right) where lines and colours are more severe.

Later, Walter Blackie would say that the elevations of the house were shown to him for approval only after the plans and interior designs had been completed (which is surely an exaggeration since the elevations are dated 1903). But the story does suggest how radically Mackintosh had broken with his predecessors. The house was designed from the inside out, with an acute awareness of the implications of this; Mackintosh scorned the conventional composition of façades. Each opening or series of openings expresses a particular interior space. The intimate curve of the master-bedroom window-bay emphasises its presence in the design of the façade. Hill House presents itself as a unity whose volumes are based on an asymmetry commanded by function. This is the basic principle of modern architecture.

Castel Orgeval

Villemoisson-sur-Orge, France, 1902-1904

Hector Guimard

A rather medieval-looking little castle, with its charmingly rustic brick-and-stone-work crowned by roofs like pointed hats, Castel Orgeval seems to have come straight out of a fairy-tale.

Hector Guimard's was a strange destiny. In his lifetime, this architect who so brilliantly represented the French version of Art Nouveau was attacked as often as he was praised. Was this because he blatantly promoted a style that he himself christened 'Guimard style'? Did the success of his Métro entrances, his sale by catalogue of decorative objects and construction elements, or his 'standardised' houses in a range of sizes and prices count against him? These entrepreneurial activities sat awkwardly with a profession in which the architect was expected to play a somewhat nobler role.

Nonetheless, Guimard's work is abundant and various, and the man himself was talented and innovative. Guimard was much more than an epigone of Brussels Art Nouveau. Within a few short years he built a series of remarkable edifices: the famous Castel Béranger in Rue La Fontaine, the École du Sacré-Cœur, the Humbert-de-Romans concert-hall, and hôtels and apartment blocks for faithful clients.

The outbreak of the Great War put an end to the Belle Époque and the carefree times that marked the beginning of the century. Nothing would ever be the same again: the moderns threw themselves into purifying forms and techniques and sung the praises of the machine age. Art Nouveau teetered on the brink of anachronism. Guimard could still show flashes of brilliance. He tried bravely to adapt to the age of reason–as shown by his office block in the Rue de Bretagne in Paris, and his own house based on a structure of "Éternit" steel tubes–but without success. The controversial idol of a brief epoch, he exiled himself to New York and died in obscurity in 1941. His work suffered the ravages of time. The entrance-halls and sculptured cast-ironwork of the Paris Métro were demolished because the administration found their upkeep too difficult. The Humbert-de-Romans concert-hall lasted only four years. His marvellous folly, the Castel Henriette was destroyed in the 1960s. Hector Guimard's reputation remains uncertain. Yet he rivals the greatest architects of the turn of the century. Was he too French? Insufficiently exotic?

Castel Orgeval belongs to his most fruitful period, which coincided with the full maturity of his art. It was designed for Achille Laurent, who dreamed that his 'Beauséjour Park' would turn Villemoisson-sur-Orge, a village south-east of Paris, into 'the Vésinet of the Orléans line'. Contemporaneous with Guimard's Castel Henriette and his villas on the Normandy coast at Cabourg and Hermanville, Castel Orgeval was halfway between a Parisian hôtel and a holiday home. Built in the middle of a large park,

Doorways and windows
are marked out
by graciously curved
stems of brick
or stone and topped
by corolla-shaped
porches. This theme
emphasises the relation
of the house to nature.
But this is a tamed
and domesticated
nature in the garden
that surrounds
the house
and isolates it from
the neighbourhood.

All openings are curved and emphasised by stone or brick in a stubborn rejection of anything even faintly orthogonal; the *style Guimard* can be seen here in its most coherent form. The house has two main façades: here the façade giving on to the garden and terrace presents the epitome of bourgeois comfort and bucolic idyll. Masonry and windows exhibit analogous curves.

surrounded by trees, it resembled some picturesque, rustic structure from the Middle Ages. Its massive pointed silhouette gave it the bucolic image of a fortified tower straight out of the pages of Victor Hugo. Standing solidly, the house rose in a single spiral barely disturbed by the orthogonal offsets. With its conical roofs of Japanese inspiration and its supple, curving balconies, it bordered on the parodic: Snow White and Perrault (the story-teller, not the architect) are not far away. The quite traditional distribution of rooms, with reception areas facing the garden and upper rooms furnished with balconies and terraces, was expressed in the disposition of openings in the façades (the structural rationalism of Viollet-le-Duc is clearly at work here). Doors and arches are rounded and highlighted by surrounds of millstone grit and white brick. Hidden behind its hedges and high trees, Castel Orgeval has an old-fashioned air of past times, of languorous *'jeunes filles en fleurs'* strolling in the summer heat. Here lies a vanished world whose perfume still lingers like that of a dried rose in an old book.

A mound of vividly coloured ceramics on the rear terrace.

Left
The façade of the Casa Batlló is brought to life by its wavy, undulating shapes, the evocation of the sea heightened by inset ceramic plates, like fish-scales. The bizarrely-shaped roof with its scaly crest has earned the nickname 'Dragon's Back'.

Casa Batlló
Barcelona, Spain, circa 1904-1906
Antoni Gaudí i Cornet

The work of Antoni Gaudí i Cornet was achieved within the particular cultural climate of the *Renaixença,* an intellectual movement that developed in Catalonia during the second half of the nineteenth century. The Renaixença struggled for the independence of the province from Spanish authority. Its torch-bearers in art and philosophy proclaimed the specificity of Catalan culture, while the movement enjoyed the support and enthusiastic patronage of ambitious, enlightened young industrialists. Among them, Gaudí found his most distinguished clients: Eusebí Güell, for whom he constructed several major buildings, Josep Batlló and Pere Milá, two associates who made their fortune in textiles, and gave their names to their *casas.*

European architecture was then going through an eclectic period. The Catalans, who were well acquainted with both John Ruskin and Viollet-le-Duc, were returning to the origins of both Gothic and Moorish art. Gaudí sought to transcend this excessively narrow framework. In Gothic architecture, he loathed the flying buttresses, which he qualified as 'crutches': he invented a parabolic arch that he modelled using string and weights, which impressed other architects and engineers of the end of the 20th century with its audacity and ingenuity. From Moorish decoration and motifs, he learnt the use of brilliantly coloured tile fragments, with which he created a primitive and fantastic bestiary, more religious than profane.

In 1904, the date at which he is presumed to have undertaken the construction of the Casa Batlló, Gaudí was in middle age and at the height of his powers. The Sagrada Família had focused his energies for more than twenty years (and he again devoted himself to it exclusively from 1914 until his tragic death in 1926). For Eusebí Güell, he created what was intended as a utopian garden suburb on the English model. Economic catastrophe ensued. But what a park!

The Casa Batlló was a synthesis of his experiments and the culmination of his art. The project was simple: to transform a small, dull building, built in 1877, into a family residence with apartments. The house is on the Passeig de Gràcia, almost at the angle with Carrer de Aragò, in what was then a fashionable district for the young bourgeoisie. From the existing building, Gaudí retained only the shell and floors, which he reinforced with cement and reinforced wooden beams. Josep Batlló had made it clear that he wanted a house still more remarkable than its neighbour, the Amatler house, built by the architect Puig i

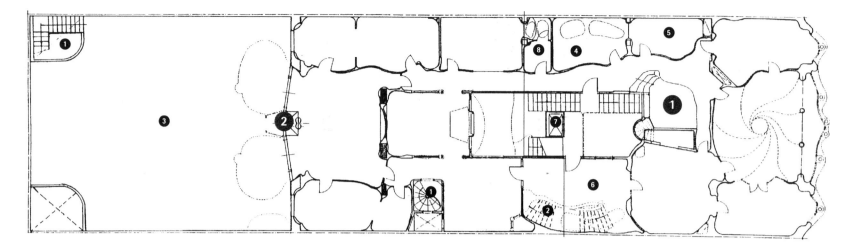

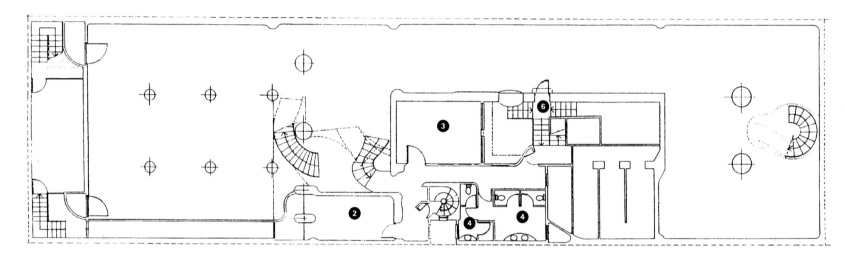

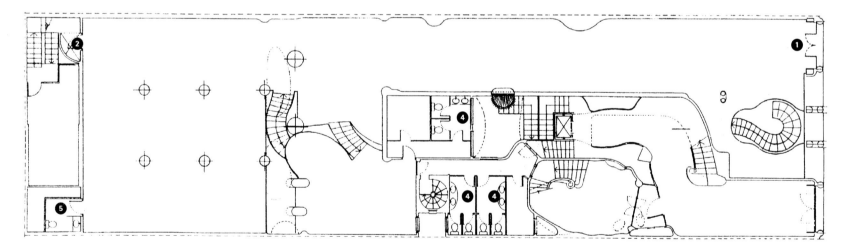

Plans of basement,
ground-floor and first floor.

Above right
Cross-section
Below
The façade on Passeig
de Grácia, its pillars
and balconies jutting
into the street.

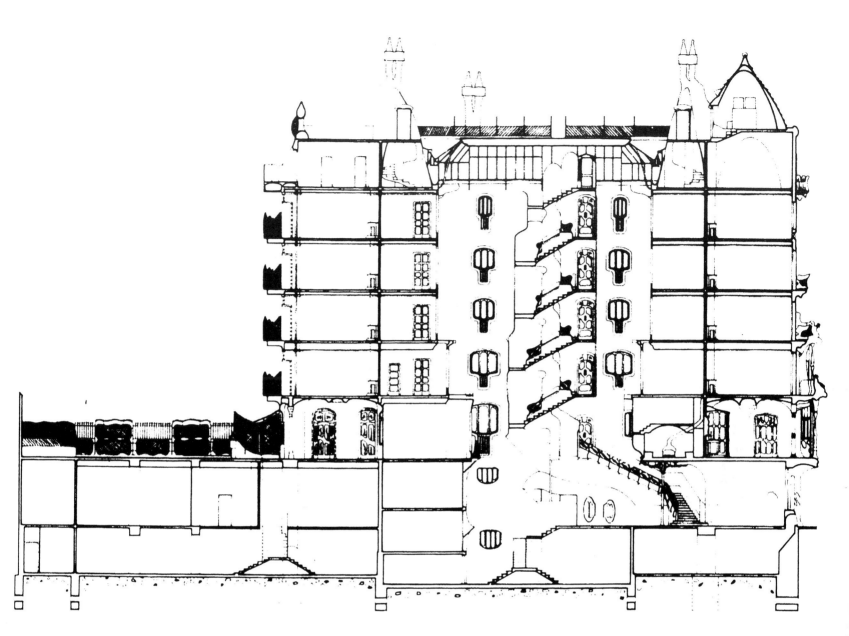

Cadalfach in 1900. Gaudí took full advantage of the great freedom of expression thus offered to him.

The new façade, resting on massive, gnarled, sinuous pillars, supports a tortuously curved platform above which is a series of balconies shaped like masks. The top storey, added on to the original structure, is made up of a series of parabolic arches of unequal height, emphasising the sinuosity of the roof line. The roof, nicknamed 'the dragon's back', is covered in glazed tiles and edged with small coloured ceramic balls. The chimneys, looking like good-natured giants, and the cross, which the now-devout Gaudí had made into his trademark, crown the building with the bright colours of ceramic fragments. The flat areas of colour on the façade afford a gentle undulation of colour from top to bottom, with nuances of blue and green in the tiles. The theme here is the sea and the movement of waves.

It is the interior of the building that marks Gaudí's break with his former approach: the style has been called 'organic', and the rooms seem almost hollowed-out, with walls and ceilings that

Two details from the banister
of the staircase leading
to the first floor.
The intimate fireplace.

Left
The lobby with its blue
and white tiles wedded
to the curves of the stairwell.

merge without angles or edges, as in a grotto. The revetment of ceramic fragments rolls and pitches, clinging to every curve and moulding, setting out the chromatic themes, which vary from room to room: shades of grey-blue in the lobby and hall, bronze and amber tones in the drawing rooms, which become paler in the bedrooms. They are counterpointed with waves of carved woodwork, emphasised by panels of coloured glass. This is a total work of art, in which Catalan *modernisme* meets Art Nouveau.

With the exception of the city of Vicenza and Palladio, there is no example of a city so strongly identified with its architect as Barcelona is with Gaudí. The city's devotion to Gaudí equals his own devotion to the city: there is hardly a poster, a postcard, or a children's game that does not bear his mark. Nothing disturbs this perfect marriage: not the *movida,* not the Olympic Games, nor the major building programme still in progress. Recent public monuments, like the Calatrava tower at Montjuic, the *Parc* Joan Miró, the Lichtenstein sculpture at the end of the harbour, or Gehry's giant fish, which stands above the marina, all appear homages and marks of allegiance to the old master.

In all this excess of glory, the Casa Batlló has not escaped its destiny. In the 1950s it was leased to the airline Iberia, then to a successful confectioner, famous for his lollipops, who carefully restored it. Today it hosts conferences and banquets, seminars and congresses, receptions and chamber-music concerts. The house has been stripped of its original furniture. The naked power of its architecture allows it to triumph in perfect dignity over these rather trivial contemporary uses. Marriages are celebrated there, perhaps offering an occasion to revive the use of the oratory where Josep Batlló had mass said for his family. Or perhaps it just gives engaged couples the chance to be videoed conforming to the morals of another age, sitting modestly in the alcove of the fireplace, under the forbidding, or complicit gaze of a chaperone.

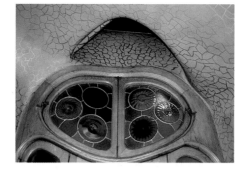

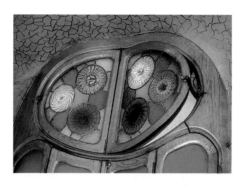

Previous pages
The wide drawing room
window looks out,
through rounded
window frames
and stained glass,
past the gnarled
and sinuous pillars
of the façade, onto
the Passeig de Gràcia.

A riot of coloured glass
and ceramics fills
the Casa Batlló,
in the woodwork,
above the doors,
in the windows
and on the ceilings.

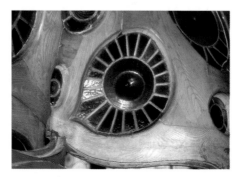

48

Demonstrators
in Leningrad
carrying the model
of the Tatlin Tower,
on May Day, 1925.

The Heroic Age
of the Moderns

At the dawn of the Roaring Twenties, a still-convalescent Europe swarmed with hordes of adventurers caught up in the feverish quest for modernity, bent on exploring all the domains of art, architecture and the city, everything that might create an environment for the advent of a new humanity. 'Change life, change the city', 'architecture or revolution', proclaimed their slogans. Machines to liberate humanity from the oppression of work became cult objects. The past was a *tabula rasa*, and architects were reinventing an art bound up with technological progress (so they said) and in tune with the great aesthetic revolutions brought about by Dada, Constructivism or De Stijl. People, ideas, and works, were in constant circulation. The fusion of all the arts was the order of the day. A school like no other, the Bauhaus brought all the disciplines together under one roof, from painting to photography, from advertising to industrial design. Its teaching staff included Gropius, Kandinsky, Itten, Klee, Breuer, Moholy-Nagy, and later Hannes Meyer and Ludwig Mies van der Rohe. The Bauhaus was shut down by the Nazis, who were, by their own lights, fully justified. These artists and architects were motivated by humane and liberal ideas and sought to improve the working of democracy. Their overriding goal was to provide housing for the greatest number of people and to search out the criteria of *existenz minimum*. Not that this prevented them from building fine houses for rich patrons, although even in these they attempted to inculcate the principles of a free, healthy and frugal life. Architecture had its moral side.

From all this great avant-garde activity, a balance-sheet was drawn up in 1932 by an unlikely couple, a young and enthusiastic curator, and a historian fresh out of Harvard. Philip Johnson, not yet an architect, and Henry-Russell Hitchcock brought together the finest examples of architectural modernity in an exhibition at the Museum of Modern Art in New York, under the banner 'International Style'. The authors followed convention in emphasising community of ideas and forms of expression, and in so doing presented a reductionist vision of their subject, one which long weighed heavily on modern architecture. The consequence was a great injustice done to modern architecture. When we return to the monuments of the time, not the least surprise is the variety of this nascent modernity. True, there are recurrent themes: liberation of the plan, liberation of space, light, health, rational construction, and the use of new materials. But under the pencils of the masters, these common denominators disappear; doctrinaire language vanishes. What is impressive in these works is their richness and their absolute originality.

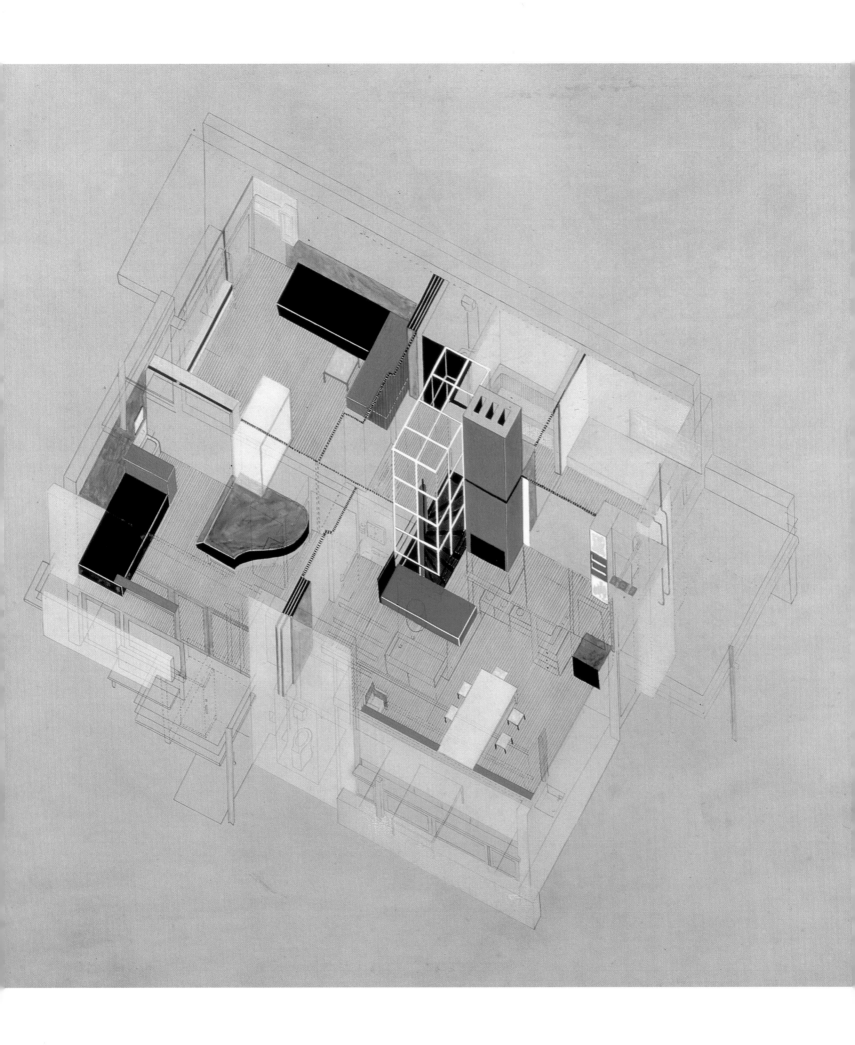

The Schröder-Rietveld House

Utrecht, Nederland, 1923-1985

Gerrit Rietveld

The Schröder House:
a modernist
doll's house,
a Constructivist
game decked out
in primary colours.

Left
Axonometric drawing
of the first floor with
its sliding partitions.

The house abutting
the last gable-end
in Prins Hendriklaan.

A room of one's own – this was one of women's first demands even before Virginia Woolf made it into a symbol of emancipation. Truus Schröder demanded it as a refuge and as compensation for an ill-matched marriage. She could hardly know that this decision would bring her into the presence of a young cabinet-maker with broad shoulders and intense eyes who would become her lifetime companion as well as a hero of modern architecture.

Truus was twenty-two when she married the lawyer Frits Schröder, to whom she bore three children. Her husband led the kind of conformist life that went with his profession. Dreamy and passionate, Truus envied the worldly life of her sister, who frequented Amsterdam literary and artistic circles. Truus had little in common with her husband: he did not share her thirst for culture, or her interest in contemporary ideas, even those which concerned the education of children. She left him three times before he died tactfully young. Of her relationship with Rietveld, we know little more than what she revealed in interviews: she met him as he delivered an armchair when she was merely engaged, and they immediately embarked upon an unconventional relationship between client and architect, meeting frequently. When she was widowed, they decided to build a house together, where she could live with her children. We know too that Truus was opposed to divorce and that Rietveld only came to live in the house after the death of his own wife. Now that the two protagonists are dead, it is hard to know what is most astonishing: their long, discreet passion, the strength of convention that drove them to create a watertight social alibi, or the fact that the building constructed continuously over more than forty years never strayed from its original conception. It kept its own kind of faith, and successive additions did nothing to diminish its coherence. For this to have happened there had to be a solid conceptual framework and a perfect accord between the architect and his client. The house is undoubtedly the fruit of an absolute collaboration between Truus Schröder and Rietveld. It was the *locus* of their complicity.

This miraculous pairing began with the choice of a site. They set out separately to look for the best place to build, and met up at the end of the weekend to find that they had both discovered the same one. It was a modest acre of land backing on to the brick gable wall at the end of a row of houses. On the edge of the town, it was set in a landscape like a painting by Ruysdael, with copses of trees in the distance and the silver threads of canals running off into the horizon. Rietveld quickly sketched out a plan, altering it to take account of Truus's reservations. From then on, despite her strong character, it seems that Truus accepted all Rietveld's suggestions, so convinced was she that together they were designing the framework for a new existence, a simple and frugal one that would break with the bourgeois lifestyle founded on appearances. Her interventions were essentially pragmatic ones, and she was therefore the perfect collaborator for the architect. Rietveld himself, a lukewarm member of the De Stijl movement, did not hold with all the theories of van Doesburg or Mondrian. A stubborn pragmatist, Rietveld had a sharper sense of realities: the fact that he trusted in models more than drawings indicates this very clearly. "This house is a chair", exclaimed the painter Claes Oldenburg when he visited it at the end of the 1980s. He certainly wasn't the first to note the striking analogy with Rietveld's famous Red and Blue chair. The house is a deliberately asymmetrical assembly of simple elements, strictly orthogonal in composition and marked out by their colours within a range intentionally reduced to primaries – blue, red, yellow – and to black, white and a few shades of grey. The building is on a modest scale. On the ground floor, the layout is straightforward, restricted by planning regulations: a hallway opening on to a little studio, a garage never used as such, which served as a workshop for Rietveld, and a spacious kitchen. The first floor, described as an attic to get round the regulations, was a vast single space, bathed in light from enormous windows,

furnished with a complex arrangement of sliding partitions to create three bedrooms and a living room. The interior of the house is full of gadgets dreamt up by Rietveld. There are shelves and drawers everywhere. There is a delivery hatch. And there is a marvellous little trick which still astonishes: a displaced support post which, when the two windows are opened, has the effect of completely eliminating the south-east corner. The colour theme, implemented to saturation point, and painted by Rietveld himself – no question of allowing someone else to intervene in the house – completes the picture. The view was subsequently disfigured by a motorway, and the fate of the house hung in the balance: Rietveld considered demolishing it, convinced that it should share the impermanence of his other constructions. Carefully restored, it stands today like a box of tricks, a brightly coloured little house resembling a child's toy, bearing witness to the innocence of modern architecture at its beginnings.

Previous pages
The first floor contains the family living spaces and bedrooms within an overall 'design' that is perfectly geometrical and absolutely practical. Nothing has escaped Rietveld's eye or paintbrush. The space can be 'open' or 'closed', thanks to an elaborate system of sliding partitions.

The south-west corner of the house with its narrow polychrome verticals.

Below
View of the south-east-facing drawing room. The window, when open, eliminates the corner.

Right
The hall and staircase to the first floor. Note the set of little drawers incorporated into the hand-rail.

The House at 10 Krivoarbatski

Moscow, USSR, 1927-1929

Konstantin Melnikov

Melnikov in front
of the Makhorka
tobacco Pavilion
at the Moscow
Agricultural Exhibition
in 1923.

Left
Melnikov's studio
with its magical play
of light through
the hexagonal windows.

Not so long ago, in a residential district of the great city of Moscow, scaffolding and a faded tarpaulin more or less concealed a ghostly silhouette. Konstantin Melnikov's house, considered one of the icons of the revolutionary period, was enduring an uncertain afterlife. No one knew whether the fact that it looked like a building site heralded its renaissance or disguised its gradual collapse. First scheduled in 1983, the restoration work had come to a standstill. Foreign businesses saw their generous offers turned down by the new authorities. The fate of this grandiose and unfortunate symbol of the vicissitudes of twentieth-century history was causing concern. Yet it had got off to a most auspicious start, in the heady days of revolutionary fervour. Even the architect's childhood seemed an edifying story. The son of a milkman, the young Melnikov was first apprenticed to an icon painter, then to a heating engineer, who spotted his talent for drawing and sent him immediately to art school. The ungrateful young man abandoned drawing for architecture, got married, and built a factory (for cars!). After the ten days that shook the world, he taught at the famous Vkhutemas and took part in the theoretical debate between Constructivists and Rationalists without taking sides. In 1925 he won the competition to design the Soviet Pavilion at the Decorative Arts exhibition in Paris (thanks to Mayakovsky, it is said). The pavilion, a Constructivist bricolage of timber and glass traversed by a huge diagonal staircase, stole the limelight from the stars of new architecture. Melnikov became the darling of Paris: Le Corbusier took him under his wing, showing him his own buildings. During a holiday in Saint-Jean-de-Luz, he took the time to plan an audacious project for a bridge with car park over the Seine. Back in Moscow, he built worker's clubs, took part in all the major competitions, and constructed his own house. But the storm was gathering. Mayakovsky committed suicide in 1930. The boat of love smashed against life's reefs. Socialist realism and the pompous celebration of power were the order of the day. Melnikov was accused of formalism, then of eccentric individualism. Unforgivable crimes. He was plagued by troubles on every side. In 1937, permission to exercise his profession was withdrawn. From then until his death in 1974, he lived the life of a recluse in his own house, the masterpiece that was now his prison, painting and meditating his former glory.

In 1927, at the height of his fame, Melnikov was financially secure thanks to the commissions for workers' clubs. Against all odds, he managed to obtain the lease on a piece of land on

The house in the Arbat
in its garden makes
a bizarre sight:
a cylinder pierced
with hexagonal
openings.

Krivoarbatski. Private leases were rare; the worthy comrade Domarev, a member of the land allocations commission, carried the day by pointing out that it was harder to find innovative projects than land. The project was indeed singular and is hard to connect to the contemporary preoccupations of the European avant-garde. The cylindrical theme is a recurrent one in Melnikov's work, and commentators have sought its origins in the work of Claude-Nicolas Ledoux, in Russian Orthodox churches, in the grain silos of the American West and even in 'le désert de Retz'. In this case, two secant cylinders make up the shell and the structure of the building. Melnikov used a traditional brick construction but varied it with diagonal columns containing a series of hexagonal openings that became windows or niches or could be plastered up according to his whim, the views, and the need for natural light. The façade on the street has a huge window extending to the top of the building, lending it a monumental dignity, reinforced by a doorway located on the axis of the two cylinders.

The floor plan meets the rites of a family life carefully organised by the architect. On the ground floor, a small hall opens on to either the family dining room or the staircase leading to the drawing room on the first floor. The door closes one entrance by opening the other, a device similar to that used by Duchamp in his Paris residence on the Rue Larrey. On the same level are the

The drawing room window opening on to the town.

Plans and cross-section of the house in the Arbat in its first version. Melnikov added a terrace on the second storey.

Right
View of the drawing room on the ground floor.

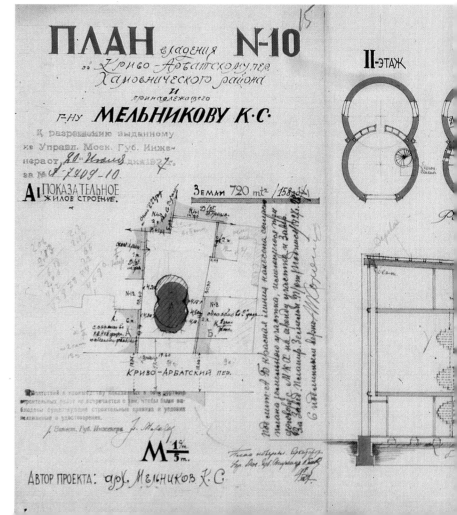

kitchen, children's workrooms, the bathroom, storage and the cloakroom. The upper floor is divided into two parts, the drawing room occupying one of the cylinders, the other containing the bedrooms. These were exclusively for sleeping; sleep was a subject on whose role and place in human existence Melnikov had very firm ideas. The bedrooms thus make up a single space, divided only by wooden partitions; the beds raised on pedestals seem to float above the ground. The bedrooms' paintwork is yellow, the dining room is blue and mauve, and the staircases light green. The workshop, on two levels, occupies the upper part of the north cylinder. Here the hexagonal openings come into their own, providing an even light throughout the workshop and demarcating a quite remarkable space. A mezzanine floor gives access to the terrace.

In its extravagance, the house of Konstantin Melnikov remains a case apart in the architecture of the century. It is modern without adhering to the canons established by the modernity of his time, anachronistic in a collectivist society, traditional in its furniture and in supporting a well-regulated domestic life. With no obvious ancestors or descendants, it stands as a pure architectural icon and a symbol of individual will. In the spring of 1997, the scaffolding and tarpaulins were removed. A museum designed by the architect Wolfgang Döring may be built on the adjacent land. The house's survival seems assured.

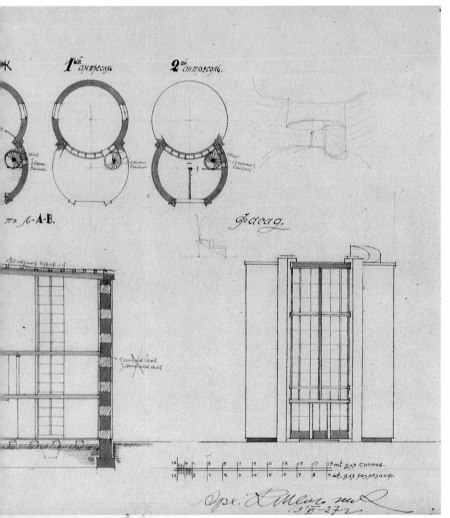

Detail of one of the
hexagonal windows.

The two interconnected
cylinders lend a gentle
aspect to the interior.
This effect is enhanced
by the muted colours
that Melnikov used.

Villa Savoye

Poissy, France, 1928-1931

Le Corbusier

The entrance
to the Villa Savoye:
a spiral staircase
and a ramp lead up
to the *piano nobile*.

The Villa Savoye was designed at the close of a decade rich in experiments. The famous 'five points' had been published at the Weißenhof exhibition in Stuttgart in 1927, and the Villa Savoye illustrates them in the most literal way. The 'five points for a new architecture' were propounded by Le Corbusier as fundamental principles, though he did not specify whether they were constructional, functional or aesthetic. It is significant that they were formulated at a time when the architect seemed to be distancing himself from the idea of 'a machine for living', and adopting more poetic images. Architecture had gone 'beyond the machine'. Five points, then: the *pilotis* (freeing space at ground level by raising the mass off the ground), the garden roof (restoring nature's ascendancy over the house), the free plan

The Villa Savoye
in its natural setting
is a pure object,
detached from
the ground and raised
above all contingency.
Le Corbusier
has applied to the letter
his 'five points for
a new architecture':
pilotis, roof terrace,
free plan, continuous
window strips, and free
façade composition.

Detail of a corner
of the drawing room
and of a door made
from a single sheet
of glass framed
in black metal.

Right
The transparent sitting-
room and the double
ramp leading
to the roof terrace.
The sitting-room
is placed between
the glass façade giving
on to the terrace
and long windows
looking over
the countryside.
In the foreground,
the *chaise-longue*
designed by
Le Corbusier,
Perriand and Jeanneret.

(eliminating load-bearing internal walls), the long horizontal window (giving free access to light), and the emancipated façade
(distinguishing façade from structure).

The Savoyes were amenable clients, rich, discreet and up to
date with the latest architecture. They knew the Church Villas
that Le Corbusier was completing in Ville-d'Avray. They turned
down a first plan as too expensive and accepted a third that was
scarcely less so. They seemed to have reconciled themselves
to the budget overruns. Le Corbusier deployed all his charm to
avoid the litigation that the structure's technical deficiencies
merited: for a long time the Villa Savoye let in water through the
windows, the ramps, and the roof terrace. The Savoyes had to
vacate the premises, and stay elsewhere, without complaining,
while the architect went about the major projects that his international status brought to him. His casual approach to unresolved
technical problems has often been held against him.

Abandoned and vandalised, the villa was taken over by the
municipality, which turned it into a youth club: it then became so
dilapidated that the municipality ordered its demolition. Saved
thanks to the intervention of André Malraux, categorised as a
building of historic interest in 1964, it was partially but inade-
quately restored. The most recent and more substantial restoration work, completed in 1997, seems to have succeeded.
Paradoxically, it has 'returned' the villa to a state of perfection that
it never had in the first place. Its original deficiencies remedied
by neoprene seals, the villa is now an ambivalent monument,
possessing both historic and novelty value. Contradicting
Gertrude Stein, it is both a museum *and* modern.

Of the features considered functional requirements by the
architect, many seem quite useless today. Now that the motor-
car is no longer an object of amazement, it seems silly to have
based the entire layout of the ground floor on the turning-circle
of the Voisin car. And are all the ramps, duplicated by a spiral
staircase, really indispensable? Is there not something terribly
aristocratic about a *piano nobile* set above a ground floor devoted
to services?

But does it matter? The *promenade architecturale* has retained
its admirable dynamism and panache. The villa is splendidly
ambiguous: extrovert in its uninterrupted rows of windows open
to the four corners of the horizon, introverted in the disposition
of its rooms, all of which give on to the patio-terrace, with the
sole exception of the bedroom of the mistress of the house.
A knowing and magnificent play of volumes, it was, thank God,
never *comme il faut*. Surrounded by a phalanx of trees that masks
the views it formerly enjoyed, the Villa Savoye is a dazzling,
virtuoso piece of work. Slightly paraphrasing Le Corbusier's
famous description, we could call it "a delayed-action poetic
object", a retroactive manifesto for the formidable freedom exer-
cised by 'the architect of the century'.

View of the drawing room
and its panoramic window looking
on to the terrace.
View from a bedroom on to the terrace
and the drawing room.
The bathroom with its tiled lounger.
The terrace and the ramps leading
to the solarium.

Following pages
The drawing room seen through
its glass façade: transparency,
reflection, refraction.

The Glass House

Paris, France, 1928-1932

Pierre Chareau and Bernard Bijvoët

Left
The reception room
and library.

Beneath a façade
of glass bricks, a house
like a drawer inserted
under a small building
in the heart
of the Faubourg
Saint-Germain.

Hailed today as an unsurpassed masterpiece, an exemplary piece of innovative, indeed visionary, architecture, the Glass House did not pass unnoticed when it was built. At the time, though, nostalgia for Beaux-Arts classicism prevailed. And its creator was a modest, gentle man with a sad smile. For whatever reason, it took several decades and its rediscovery by British hi-tech enthusiasts for the house to become a monument to modernity. It has to be said that Chareau never seems to have felt the irresistible attraction for architecture that makes brilliant careers. A contemporary of all the great movements of the time, he counted himself among the *meubliers*, the name then given to furniture- designers, and the *ensembliers* (interior designers) halfway between the society commission and the luxury design shop. Chareau's other ventures into architecture were few and far between. They include a golf clubhouse at Chateauvallon, a little country house for a dancer, a bungalow for a couple of women artists, and the studio-house he built for Motherwell. Built at the end of his life, the latter was, alas, demolished by a developer: at East Hampton, Long Island, a building resembling a military hutment, even when designed by an obscure great architect, was unlikely to survive the pressure on real estate.

There was, then, nothing to suggest the posthumous glory awaiting Chareau. Once again, we see that great architecture

The great library:
the wall of 'Nevada'
glass bricks spreads
a beautiful light
over furniture designed
by Chareau, sofas
and fan-shaped nest
of tables. The studded
rubber floor-covering
is original.

requires a great client. Doctor Dalsace and his wife Annie were exemplary clients: not only were they enlightened members of the upper middle class and patrons of the arts, but they also had talent enough to recognise and value Chareau and place complete trust in him. They were never to regret it.

Seemingly straightforward, the task they gave him was actually a delicate one: to transform a small building in the Faubourg Saint-Germain between a courtyard and a garden into a house that would reconcile the needs of family life and the exercise of the doctor's profession. This apparently attractive project was complicated by the fact that the third floor of the building was occupied by sitting tenants.

It required considerable audacity at the time to imagine placing the third floor on high supports and to slide into the freed space a kind of box-drawer constituting the shell of the house. Chareau completed his prestidigitation with another original solution: in order to provide light for the lower levels, he invented a beautiful façade in 'Nevada' glass bricks, an idea that would be adopted by many other architects, including Le Corbusier. These two major innovations alone would have been a significant architectural advance. But that was not all. The exposed metal structure opened up vast, high spaces into which the façade threw an unreal

The study overlooking the garden. The wooden desk with metal frame was designed by Chareau.

Right
A bedroom overlooking the garden.

light, by night as well as day thanks to spotlights on the exterior. In his fittings for the house, Chareau dreamt up some astonishing gadgets: we mention only the mechanical ventilation shutters, and the hand-rails that were also bookshelves. With remarkable intuition, he anticipated ideas that would decades later be championed by the Archigram group, Cedric Price and other torch-bearers of English hi-tech. For example, he made the energy conduits visible and accessible, for the simple reason that they were likely to require replacement well before the structure of the house. Better still, with the collaboration of his colleague, the ironworker Dalbet, Chareau invented an industrial aesthetic which employed materials unknown in domestic architecture, humble materials chosen for their texture and particular qualities, with scrupulous refinement. Young architects at the end of this century are still amazed at the perforated sheet-metal and the moiré effects it produces, the narrow metal duckboards of the staircases, the studded natural rubber on the floors and the whole play of squares and hatching which lends the space its beautiful depth. Without ever having imagined his Glass House as a model or a prototype, something which would surely have gone against his convictions, Chareau conceived a building which has proved to be a major influence for the second half of the century.

View of the main
drawing room beneath
the mezzanine, looking
towards the garden:
the room is a meeting
place of light from
courtyard and garden.

Left
The staircase. It leads
to a *piano nobile*
in the best traditions
of the Parisian hôtel.
The open steps
are attached to
two metal beams.
The hand-rail, a simple
metal rod, curving back
on itself at the top,
defines the space.

Tugendhat House

Brno, Czechoslovakia, 1928-1930

Ludwig Mies van der Rohe

Implacable geometry and sumptuous materials: view across the living room reflected from the onyx wall, with smoked glass commode, cruciform pillars in chromed steel and, in the background, the curved partition in macassar.

The story of one of the uncontested architectural masterpieces of the century begins with a romantic idyll. Grete and Fritz were young and in love. They belonged to Brno's comfortable middle class. Grete's dowry included a fine piece of land in the Cernà Pole district, on the side of a gentle hill, with a magnificent view over the town and the Spilberk castle. Even before they were married, they dreamed of building a house there, where they would live with the two children that Grete had from her first marriage. One of their friends, the art critic Edouard Fuchs, lived in Berlin in a brick house designed in the neo-classical style of Karl Friedrich Schinkel by a young man called Ludwig Mies van der Rohe, who was still under the influence of his master, Peter Behrens. This was the architect to whom they planned to offer their project.

Mies van der Rohe was then at the summit of his European career. He was the Vice-President of the Werkbund, and he had

Cross-section.

Floor plans:
ground floor, first floor
with living rooms,
top floor
with bedrooms.

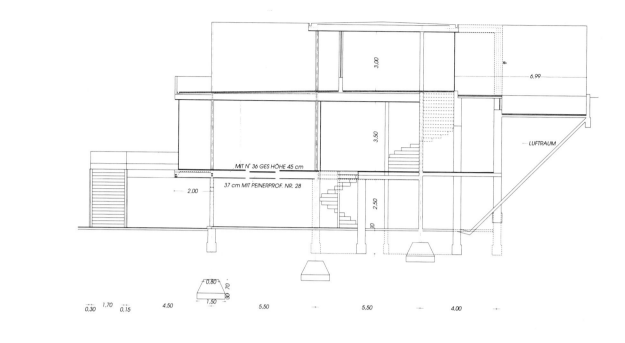

MIT N° 36 GES HÖHE 45 cm

37 cm MIT PEINERPROF. NR. 28

LUFTRAUM

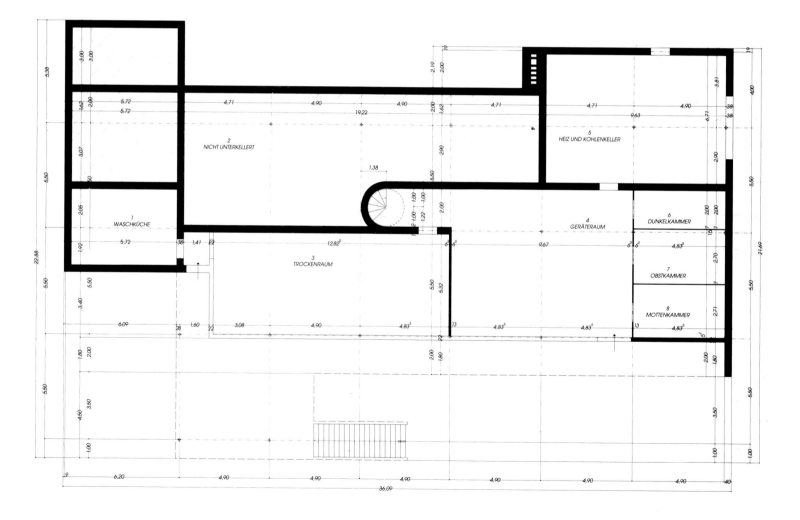

1 WASCHKÜCHE
2 NICHT UNTERKELLERT
3 TROCKENRAUM
4 GERÄTERAUM
5 HEIZ UND KOHLENKELLER
6 DUNKELKAMMER
7 OBSTKAMMER
8 MOTTENKAMMER

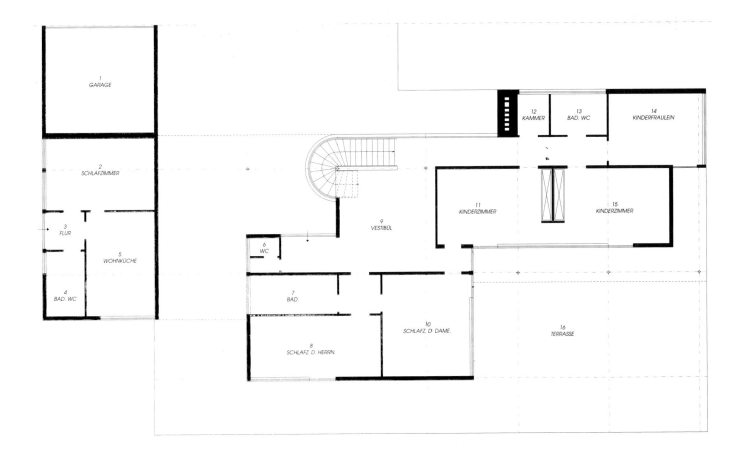

1 GARAGE
2 SCHLAFZIMMER
3 FLUR
5 WOHNKÜCHE
4 BAD. WC
6 WC
7 BAD.
8 SCHLAFZ. D. HERRN.
9 VESTIBÜL
10 SCHLAFZ. D. DAME.
11 KINDERZIMMER
12 KAMMER
13 BAD. WC
14 KINDERFRAULEIN
15 KINDERZIMMER
16 TERRASSE

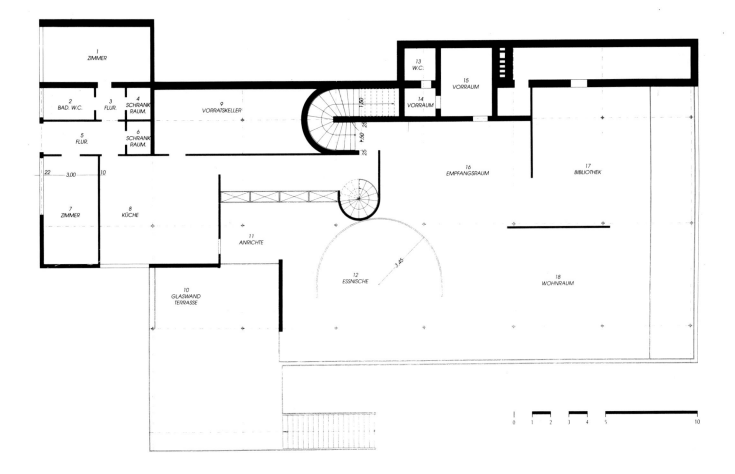

1 ZIMMER
2 BAD. W.C.
3 FLUR.
4 SCHRANK RAUM.
5 FLUR.
6 SCHRANK RAUM.
7 ZIMMER
8 KÜCHE
9 VORRATSKELLER
10 GLASWAND TERRASSE
11 ANRICHTE
12 ESSNISCHE
13 W.C.
14 VORRAUM
15 VORRAUM
16 EMPFANGSRAUM
17 BIBLIOTHEK
18 WOHNRAUM

22   3.00   10

1.50   25

1.50   25

3.45

0 1 2 3 4 5   10

just completed the housing development at Weißenhof in Stuttgart, which had brought together the leading lights of the European avant-garde, from Gropius to Scharoun, from Le Corbusier to Mart Stam and J.J.P. Oud. He was preparing his celebrated German pavilion for the 1929 International Exhibition in Barcelona. This was the project he described to the Tugendhats at their first meeting in the autumn of 1927. Grete was enthusiastic. At first, Mies van der Rohe hesitated, doubting whether he could find a workforce adequate to his ambitions in this provincial town. Then he came to Brno and was reassured. He liked the site. In December 1927, the project took shape. At the end of 1930, the Tugendhats moved in.

The house is built into the slope of the hill, and from the road, its only visible part is the upper level. This is divided into two masses that are simple parallelepipeds spanned by a single roof: one of them encloses the services and garage, the other the front door and the bedroom level. Between the two blocks there is an enclosed opening with a view over the town. A semi-cylindrical opalescent glass panel marks out the entrance and illuminates the hall with its travertine floor. All along the corridor, the distribution of rooms follows an absolutely traditional pattern. The south-facing rooms give onto a terrace overlooking the garden. Mies van der Rohe fully revealed his art in the 700 m² space of the lower level, which – apart from the services – leaves a free space of 15 metres by 24. The east and south façades are open to the landscape through three by five metres glass windows. Two of them can be lowered into the floor by a simple mechanism. There is no interruption between interior and exterior; the east-facing winter garden provides a gentle transition. Nor are there any interior limits. The two dividing panels, one a gold, red and onyx partition, the other a semicircle of macassar, mark out the living spaces – living room, area for eating, office and library – without separating them. The materials are simple and sumptuous: wood, onyx, ivory-white linoleum, unbleached silk curtains, wool rugs, all orchestrated by the discreet verticals of cruciform, chrome-plated columns. The furniture, designed either for the house itself or for the Barcelona pavilion, is positioned with all the rather severe precision of which Mies van der Rohe was capable. Every little detail, door-handles, skirting-boards, metal fittings – God is in the details, Mies used to say – was designed with obsessive care. The lower level contained storage space and the most sophisticated equipment of the time: central heating and air-conditioning with humidifiers, and the electromagnetic system to raise and lower the windows. In all its Spartan luxury, the Tugendhat House remains the ideal of the modern architecture of its time.

But events in the outside world were taking an alarming turn. The Bauhaus, then directed by Mies van der Rohe, was closed down by the Nazis in 1933. In 1938, Mies took over the running of the architecture department of the Armour Institute in Chicago

Main entrance to the house with opalescent glass wall. Detail of door onto the terrace made from a single sheet of glass framed in metal. The tubular chromed steel furniture was designed by Mies van der Rohe and is known as 'Brno'.

and did not return to work in Germany until the 1950s. The Tugendhats were progressive Jews. When Hitler annexed the Sudetenland, they made their decision. They left for Venezuela (not without first protecting the onyx wall with a layer of plaster). The house entered a dark period: it was requisitioned by the Gestapo, then by the technical section of Messerschmidt. After the German defeat, it was the turn of the Soviet cavalry to damage the floors. The house was ransacked, the windows boarded up. Later still it was used by a dance school, and as a convalescent home by a children's hospital.

In the 1960s, Grete Tugendhat returned to claim her property. It was tactfully suggested to her to make a gift of it to the state, which would ensure its upkeep. Restoration, begun in 1980, was frequently interrupted, and it was not until 1989 that the house regained some of its former splendour. The town of Brno is making efforts to restore it to its original appearance.

But can one actually live in the Tugendhat House? This was the provocative question posed by a critic in 1931. Grete and Fritz Tugendhat gave their own answer. Grete affirmed that the fluidity of the space was truly liberating. Fritz told of how, muffled up against the cold by the open window on a clear winter's day, he felt as though he was in Davos in the Swiss Alps. After spending a lot of time in the house, a recent witness claimed that it had a spiritual influence. Unaffected though he was by public opinion, Mies van der Rohe would no doubt have appreciated the compliment.

Right
The terrace
on the bedroom level
with hand-rail
and bench following
the same curve.
The dining area
is screened by
a curved partition
in macassar.

Following pages
General view
of the drawing room:
the Barcelona chairs
in front of the wall
of onyx from
the Atlas Mountains.
The female bust
by Georg Kolbe
is a distant cousin
of the 'Aurora' naiad
of the 1929
Barcelona Pavilion.

Pages 92 and 93
General view
of the winter garden
and the east
and south windows
looking over the park
and town respectively.

The Tugendhat House
in winter.

Between Avant-Garde and Tradition

Lambrate.
Saul Steinberg, 1971.

Left
Police file.
Berlin, 1935.

In the aftermath of the Great Depression, in the shadow of rising totalitarianism, the modern movement had attained its age of reason, and gained some degree of acceptance. Its architects now abandoned polemics to devote themselves to their work. Neo-Classicism and regionalism, having weathered the storm of modernity, made a comeback – and not only, as some like to believe, under authoritarian regimes. The 1937 Universal Exhibition in Paris marked the high point of this return to order. The exhibits were divided between monumental architecture, embodying authority in all its pomp, and rural, folkloric *Heimatstil* aimed at the masses. Only industries, confident of their own future, displayed in their elegant pavilions the latest technological feats of a tamed modernism, which everyone was convinced could serve only peaceful ends. But anxiety was growing, and progressives, Jews and 'decadent' artists were leaving Europe for safer havens. Their anxiety, of course, was all too well founded. A second great conflict, even more destructive than the first, was about to create the *tabula rasa* of which architects had rashly dreamed. Europe in ruins would, for two decades after the Second World War, demand massive reconstruction work. Alas, the price of this was 'modern' architecture of little quality, hastily designed and built. These times were not conducive to the flourishing of a happy and serene domestic architecture. The houses that embodied the spirit of the age did not invariably survive the catastrophe; those that did, the avatars of history, were the products of miraculous chance or what was sometimes an anachronistic individual act of will.

After the war, architects involved in mass production gave only the most fleeting thought to any particular house. Architecture recovered its energy and confidence only at the end of the 1950s. And the balance-sheet for the preceding years is a very mixed one.

Villa Girasole

Marcellise, near Verona, Italy, 1929-1935

Engineer: Angelo Invernizzi

Architect: Ettore Fagiuoli

Mechanical Engineer: Romolo Carapacchi

A villa with a
modernist silhouette,
its terrace crowned
with a pergola
and belvedere,
amid the vines
and cypresses
of the Veronese
countryside.
It revolves!

"The least you can expect of a sculpture is that it shouldn't move." Salvador Dalí's scandalised reaction to one of Alexander Calder's early mobiles came too late. After the Futurists, the panegyrists of speed, came Giacometti, Duchamp, and Picabia with their poetic recreation of a world in movement. The railway, the motor car, and the aeroplane had come into existence. The machine was in motion. What would Dalí, 'the concentric eccentric', have said about the Girasole house?

Its inventor, Angelo Invernizzi, had trained in naval engineering in Genoa and in civil engineering in Padua. He set up in business at Genoa, and carved out a highly successful career. The most prominent surviving marks of this success are the clock tower he built with Marcello Piacentini, Mussolini's favourite architect, and a daring car park, which for the first time used a helicoidal ramp (still in service today). On the land he had acquired in the village of his childhood, he decided to build a country house. The spirit of the time, or perhaps the daily spectacle of the port of Genoa, with its lofty cranes and majestic gantries, helped him to an extraordinary idea, which involved applying in the domestic sphere a technology tried and tested in another. The result was a house that revolved so as to position itself relative to sun and wind at the most appropriate, enjoyable and effective angle for every season.

The foundation is of reinforced concrete in the form of a drum. A circular tower constructed of Wierendel columns and beams is set on an axle and moves around a horizontal ring with wheels. A circular platform carried on railway bogies and moving around three rails uses the power of two three-horsepower engines. The result is a house consisting of two wings joined to the tower at an angle of 90° that can rotate at a speed of six millimetres per minute. Between the sombre verticals of the cypresses, the landscape slips slowly by, with its flat cultivated terraces, the vineyard, the cherry orchard, and the olive grove. Facing inland, the terrace is almost on a level with the park. Looking down, it overhangs a sloping garden, with a bean-shaped

Plans of living
and sleeping floors.

Below right
The magnificent
simplicity of the
construction,
with Wierendel
pillars and beams
and concrete flooring.
Above right
The building
in its finished state.

Axonometric drawing
of the structure
and machinery
for rotation.

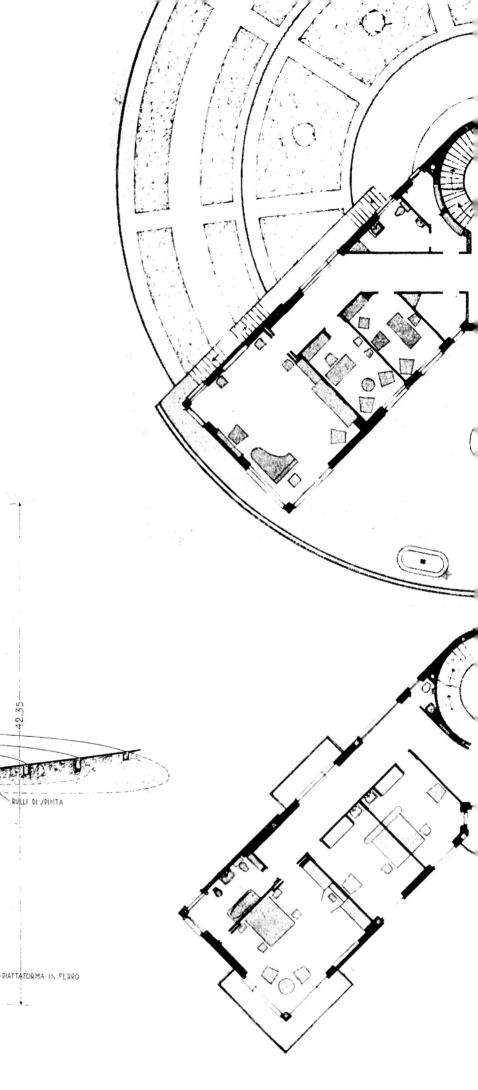

CARRELLI MOTORI

RULLI DI SPINTA

42.35

INGRESSO

PIATTAFORMA IN FERRO

RALLA

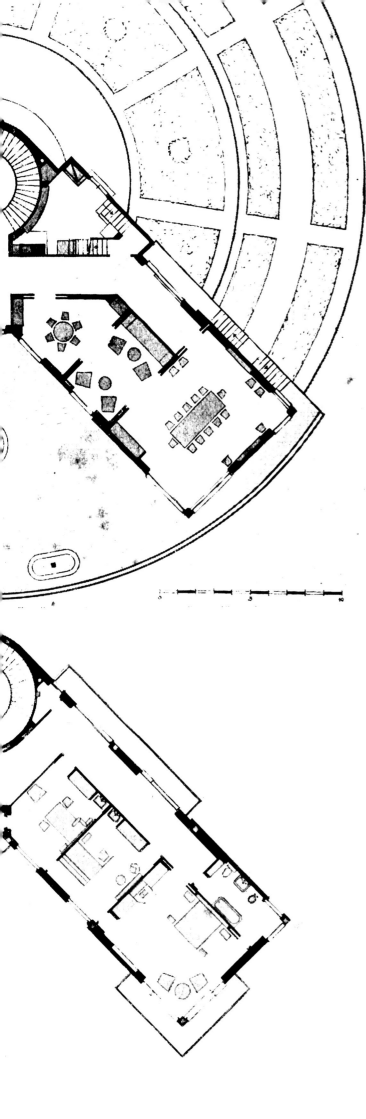

swimming pool and a diving-board that would not have looked out of place in Ove Arup's Penguin Pool.

The Girasole ('Sunflower') united two aesthetics that rarely come together. The architect, Ettore Fagiuoli, had clearly made concessions to the Neo-Classicism and Mussolinian pomp in vogue at the time, as evidenced by his twisted columns flanking the entrance and his marble revetments. But the body of the house obviously owed much more to the engineer and followed the principles of a rather archaic industrial aesthetic – with mechanical devices borrowed from railways and docks – combined with a lightness and grace still surprising today. The aluminium alloy plates, screwed down (by hand) like those of an aircraft fuselage, whose tolerance of expansion and contraction creates a kind of cushioned effect, dulling reflected light, would not look out of place on a late 20th century building. Rooms in the living quarters are distributed along two corridors joined by entrance halls at the exit of the lift. The living rooms open on to the terrace through wide windows or glass doors; corner rooms have a large balcony. The Villa Girasole remains remarkably modern: the sharply defined, black-bordered metal frames and fixtures, the electric shutters operated from a bedside control panel in the master bedroom, the bathrooms decorated with multicoloured mosaics, none of these have aged in the slightest. The engineer's daughter, Lidia Vacari Invernizzi, has maintained the house with great care. She comes to the house in early summer and autumn. She rotates it by a few degrees to ensure the mechanism still works, always afraid that it may stop for good. Lidia Invernizzi fears for the future. The growing reputation of the Villa Girasole in architectural circles should guarantee its future, but official recognition has been slow to come. Yet the house stands as a formidable monument to an epoch, a unique symbol of the intense – and no doubt somewhat naïve – faith in progress and technology that has irradiated the century as a whole. Folly, *machine célibataire*, or Daliesque poetic object, the Villa Girasole is a vision of utopia realised in metal and concrete.

The terrace between the two wings, rotated here to the south and overlooking the slope down to the valley.

Below:
the building rests on bogies and rails set into concrete beds.
Opposite:
the Wierendel system on the staircase.

The exterior is faced with aluminium panels. They are simple to assemble and provide a relatively flat surface.

Left
The villa stands
on a drum
of reinforced concrete
built into the slope,
with an entrance
at the bottom
and an ambulatory
on the upper level
looking over the park.

Detail of the door
and Bakelite
light-switch.

Above right
A bedroom
on the upper floor,
with period furniture.

Tiling with modernist
design at the end
of a corridor.

Villa Mairea

Noormarkku, Finland, 1938-1939

Alvar Aalto

A villa of dazzling white, tempered by the wooden balconies, the dark mass of the studio, and the gilded horizontals of the blinds. View of the south-west corner with the dark shape of the studio above the winter garden.

By the mid-1930s, Alvar Aalto had already produced a notable body of work that included two monuments of modernity, a sanatorium at Païmio and a library at Vijpuri, both in Finland. Aalto was younger than Le Corbusier, Mies van der Rohe and Walter Gropius, and he did not, as they did, need polemics and manifestos to win over his contemporaries. Finland was then a young country proud of its independence, open to new ideas and social debate. Moreover, Aalto had quickly managed to free himself from the shackles of doctrine and to find his own language, a language close to the concerns of his fellow citizens. His interest in local culture and his use of natural materials also played a part in his early recognition.

Of the partisans Aalto had won over to his cause, the closest to him were the Gullichsens. Harry Gullichsen was a young and

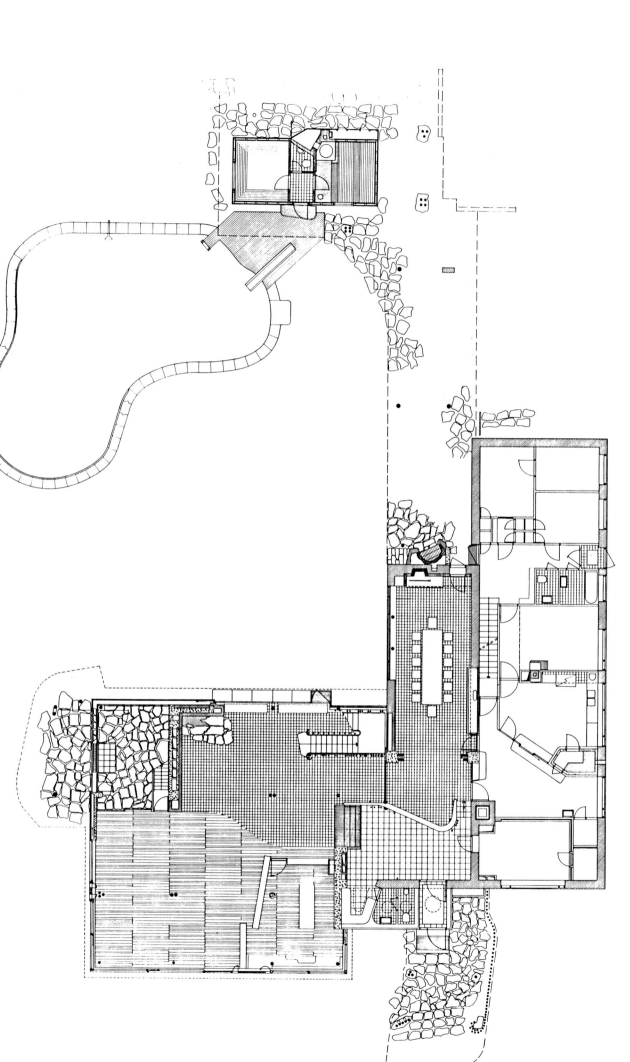

Previous pages
The villa with its
projecting windows
seen through
the pine trunks.

Plans of the ground
floor and first floor,
showing the reception
areas and service wing
on the ground floor
separated from
the more private
first floor.

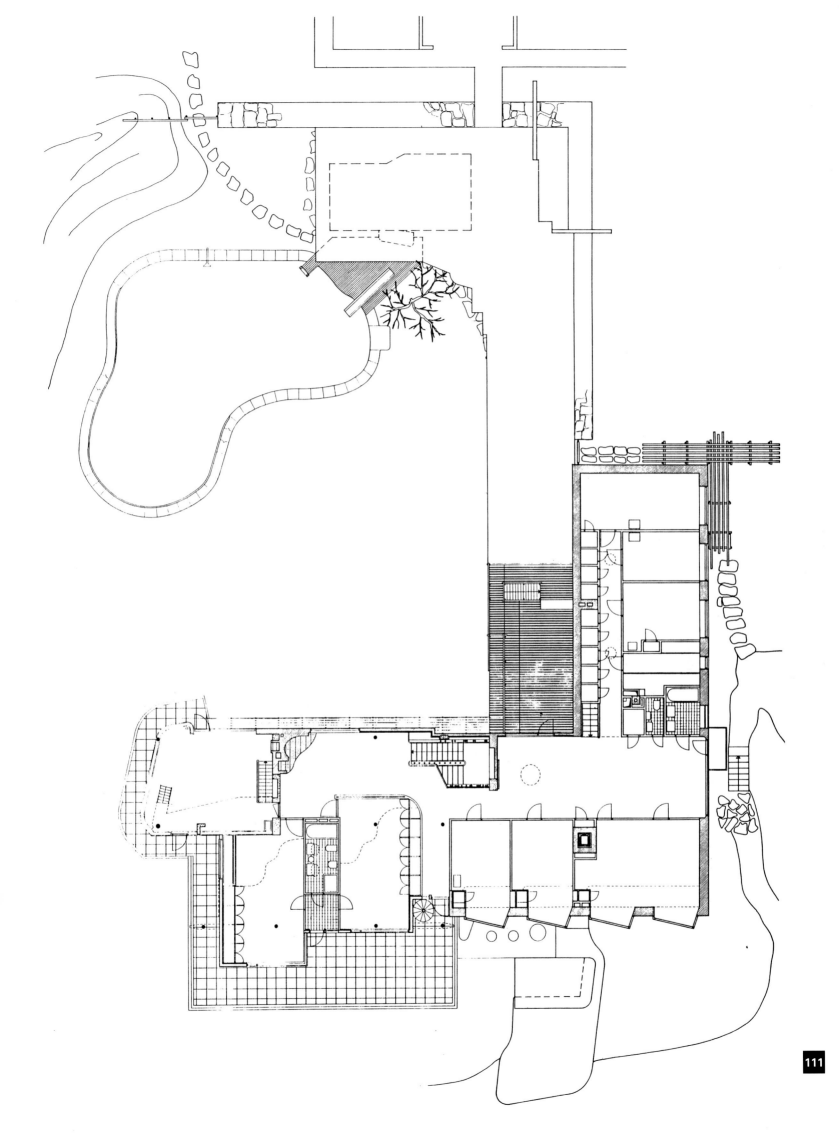

prosperous businessman in the timber industry; Maire was a great enthusiast of modern art. They became friends with Aino and Alvar Aalto. The two couples exchanged ideas, realised that they shared the same ideals, and together founded a movement that they called Hairal, an anagram of their four Christian names. They formed a company called Artek which produced (and indeed still produces) furniture and objects designed by Aino and Alvar. Like the Russian Constructivists, who wanted architecture to become a 'social capacitator', they believed that architecture should create social harmony, should literally 'build' the world of the future. Villa Mairea was to be the model.

It was in Noormarkku, in the west of the country, a short distance from the Gulf of Bothnia, that the Gulichsens chose to build their house; the land belonged to Maire's family, the Ahlströms. The site was enormous. The Ahlström manor-house stood on the edge of a pine forest overlooking a gentle, lawned slope flanked by a long pergola. The Villa Mairea is built on a low, rocky eminence to the east of the larger building. Unlike the manor house, which faces open country, the villa is surrounded by the tall, dark trunks of pine trees, and slowly becomes visible as one approaches it. Built on an L-shaped plan (which was closed off by the addition of a sauna), the villa is fronted by a long, white façade. An elegant canopied porch marks the entrance. There are four projecting windows on the first floor, and high ground-floor windows with varnished wooden blinds. On the west side of the roof, a dark wooden tower overlooks the terrace, on which there is a bean-shaped pool that was widely copied in the 1950s.

The architectural language of the villa is modern, but tempered by an organic quality; its forms are soft, and it uses a variety of distinctive materials on a background of white roughcast. Wood is used either in natural forms – planks of untreated wood support the porch and mark out the motif on the east façade – or in slats, vertical strips and varnished ceilings. The chimney of worked stone has a blue ceramic surround, a decoration that Aalto often used.

As well as being a family home, the house had another, more noble role: it was to be a meeting-place for friendly debates and discussions. The free and open plan of the ground-floor, with its separate drawing rooms, its library, its dining room and long dining table, and its winter garden, all of them fluid spaces, reveals Aalto's skill in merging intimacy and conviviality. Aalto was not greatly interested in the omnipresent, uniform, external landscape; his chief concern was the lighting of the interior, whose colour and intensity he controlled by the use of screens, drapes and filters. The light plays subtly on the wood and metal of the piano, on the furniture, the sculptures, and the staircase, which stands like an object in its own right, flanked on both sides by rounded wooden poles. This intimate ambience is heightened by the works of art that Maire chose with care: a Poliakov canvas,

Above: the office
with steps leading up
to the studio.

Above left
The dining room
with a tapestry
by Fernand Léger.

Below left
The fireplace corner
in the drawing room,
with a Degas sculpture
of a dancer.

Following pages
View of the main
staircase in the drawing
room, and the main
entrance.

Details of door-handles
and hand-rail
of staircase.

The unusual piano,
like some three-legged
animal out of science-
fiction.

Right
Light filtered through
the blinds creates
a golden penumbra.

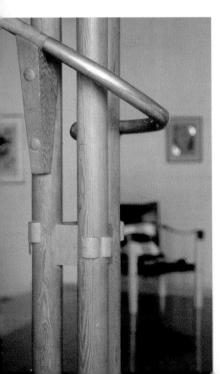

a Degas bronze, and a Léger tapestry. In the Villa Mairea, the fusion of the arts became a reality.

In the summer of 1939, the Gullichsens moved into this embodiment of hope-filled modernity. In November, the Soviet army invaded Finland. The dream was shattered. Mairea returned at the end of the war. But times had changed: the house was too big, the nearest town too far away. The house was used only occasionally, for family reunions. More than fifty years on, Kristian Gullichsen can still remember the moment when, as a little boy, lying on the parquet floor of the drawing room, staring at the ceiling, he decided to abandon his decision to be a bus driver and to become an architect.

The Villa Malaparte perched on its eyrie on the Massullo headland.

Villa Malaparte

Capri, Italy, 1938-1942

Adalberto Libera (initial sketch)

Curzio Malaparte

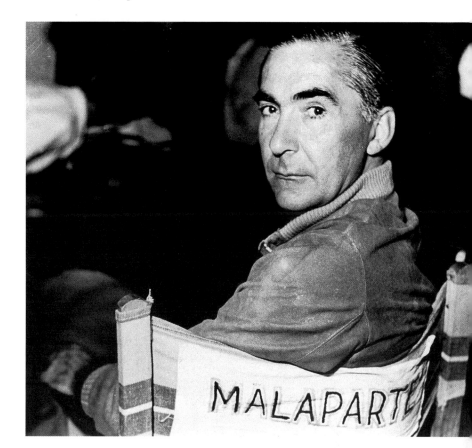

Until recently, Curzio Malaparte was remembered for his protean literary work, his almost excessively adventurous life, and his extraordinary political career; he was at various times a regionalist – *strapaesano* – a Fascist, a Communist, and a Maoist. His outspokenness cost him dear; he was exiled and imprisoned more than once. Man of letters, poet, essayist, reporter, chronicler, magazine proprietor, playwright and film-maker, Malaparte was active in many fields. And it is now recognised that the Malaparte house on the island of Capri was largely his own work; it had hitherto been unquestioningly attributed to the architect Adalberto Libera. The Casa Malaparte was designed and built by the writer with the help of the master mason Adolfo Amitrano. Libera drafted only the initial blueprint, used to obtain a building permit. This belated revelation has provoked something of a scandal in the corporatist world of Italian architecture. There was some indignation that the masterpiece of an era was 'architecture without an architect' – that is, created without the intervention of a properly trained, properly qualified professional.

Malaparte used to say that
he had only constructed
the landscape: three views
of the Bay of Matromania
and the Faraglioni rocks.

Right
The roof terrace with
its curved screen wall.

But there is no getting round it: the chameleon-like Malaparte was also an architect!

On his first transfer from the island of Lipari to the island of Ischia, where he was again exiled in 1934, Malaparte nursed the project of building a house on the Bay of Naples. This idea was left behind when he moved to Forte dei Marmi, an elegant, cosmopolitan resort on the Tuscan coast. In 1937, at the time of the great commemorations of imperial Rome, he landed on Capri with his friend Tamburi and a 'flock of diplomats'. Capri is an island of fishermen, cherished by the Emperor Tiberius, who built a few villas there (including the Villa Jovis). It was rediscovered at the beginning of the century by nature-loving artistocrats. Galeazzo Ciano, the young and talented Minister of Foreign Affairs and son-in-law of Il Duce, liked to stay there. He was not alone in this. Malaparte could resist neither the wild, rugged beauty of the Massullo headland nor the proximity of the powerful. For an unbeatable price he acquired a barren piece of land, where construction was apparently neither possible nor permitted. Libera's blueprint and the influence of the Minister of Education, Bottai, who had overall control of protected sites, obtained for him the supposedly unobtainable building permit. According to the official report, the building was to be invisible (!). In the following years, Malaparte served in the army on the French front, then led the wandering life of a war correspondent, in Romania, the Ukraine, Yugoslavia, Finland, and the Russian front. Between two of these missions, he came to Capri, visited the site, consulted colleagues, took decisions, changed his mind, and became impatient at the slow pace of the building work, which the prevailing conditions exacerbated. The house filled his thoughts and swallowed up all the money he made from his articles. So impatient was he that, well before building was completed, he moved into the guest rooms. It was there that he finished his novel *Kaputt* in 1943.

Libera's blueprint, by obtaining the building permit, had established a strict framework that Malaparte could not change without jeopardising his project. There is no evidence that he wanted to; he liked the location, on a cliff whose shape appealed to him, and he appreciated the plan's geometrical rigour. However, the two liberties he did take with the original design radically altered the house. In order to create an entrance in the longitudinal axis and construct the terrace and the steps leading up to it, which were an explicit reference to the terrace and steps of the Church of the Annunciation in Lipari, he enlarged the house's foundations. This gave the house its characteristic profile and transformed the ground plan: Libera had intended the rooms to be distributed off a long lateral corridor, but Malaparte wanted an axial distribution, more in keeping with his idea of an antique *domus*. However, Mastro Amitrano refused to countenance an entrance modelled on the *vomitoria* of ancient Greek amphitheatres; his arguments were reinforced when a few

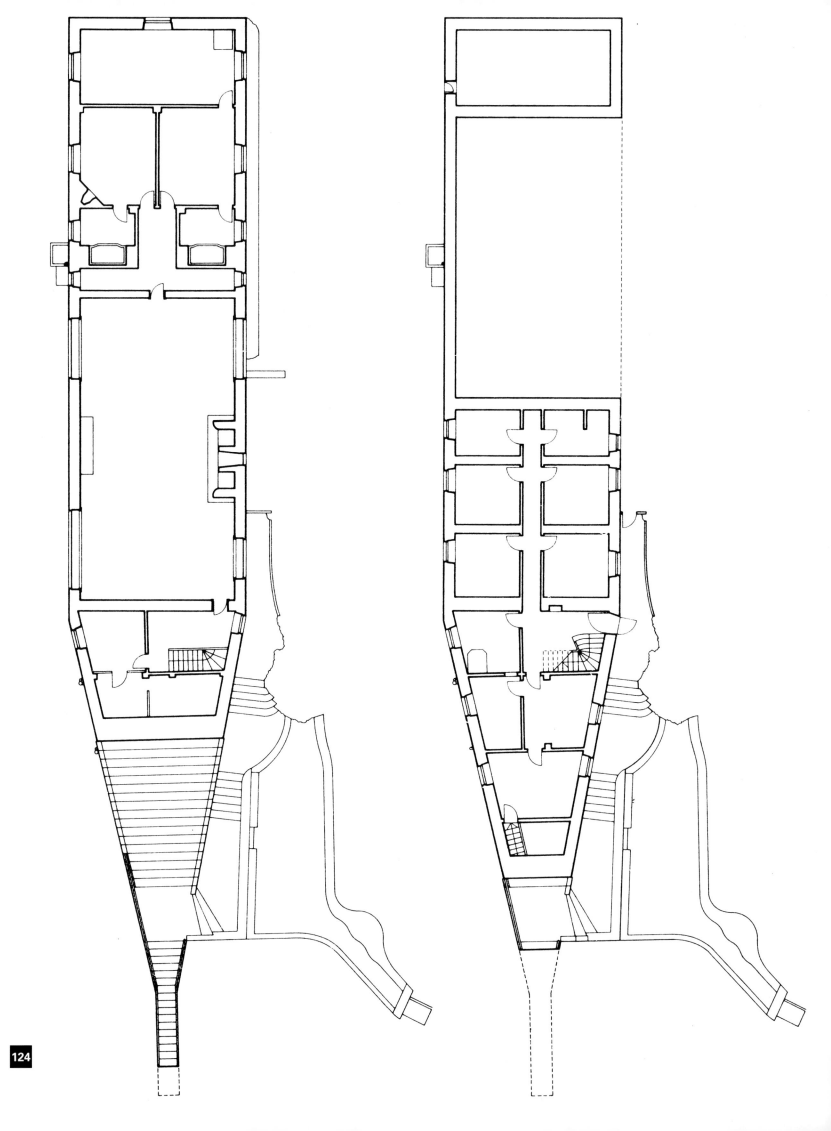

Detail of the locks
on the main gate.

Previous pages
Classical theatricality:
stone steps cut
into the rocks
and blood-red walls.

Left
Floor plans: ground
floor, drawing room
and bedrooms.

downpours revealed the full absurdity of the idea. The *vomitorium* was blocked up, and the wide steps became the only access to the terrace. This is an empty, open space, whose original balustrade was soon removed; it now has a rather clumsy curved parapet wall, for which Tamburi provided the design. The entrance was moved to the north-west façade, and the first floor was bizarrely served by a boxed-in staircase – a remarkable piece of clumsiness, this, an architectural howler. The error is quickly forgotten when one enters the *atrium*, a huge, bare room, whose size Malaparte would proudly stress to his friends by taking fifteen strides before turning and shouting: "Fifteen metres, that's how long it is!" It is here that Malaparte expressed his sense of place: four wide windows of unequal size, framed in chestnut, provide the most beautiful cameos over the Bay of Matromania to the north-east and the Faraglioni rocks to the south-west. "I didn't construct the house," Malaparte said to Field-Marshal Rommel, who may or may not have visited him here shortly before El Alamein, "but I did construct the landscape". The atrium is almost bare of furniture. There is a heavy table set on salomonic wooden pillars and benches each supported by two fluted columns. A console table stands by the huge fireplace, whence the household gods, too, had a view over the landscape, through a little glass opening in the middle of

the hearth. Here one can get a glimpse of what Malaparte meant when he talked of surrealism having its origins in Greek and Roman antiquity. The Casa Malaparte is like one of De Chirico's metaphysical objects. The modernity espoused by the writer is merely a facade in this minimalist geometry. Besides, how can a building be 'modern' with walls eighty centimetres thick? Perched on the edge of an abyss, out of time, like some austere, formidable casemate for a melancholy sentinel, the building is the narcissistic equivalent of the prison that Malaparte wanted to live in. In an article for *Corriere della Sera* on 18 October 1940, he wrote: "The Parthenon is undoubtedly the most perfect metaphysical machine that men have ever made. Or perhaps it is also a great marble cage, the prison of the little bird Zeus..." The Casa Malaparte, a sublime prison that echoes the silence of eternity? Hardly. There are worse fates than being condemned to live there.

The drawing room with its Spartan furniture: a console and two solid wooden tables on stone plinths.

Left
Malaparte's mistresses were accommodated in a bedroom with tiled floor and fireplace and en-suite marble bathroom.

Malaparte's office and library as it is today.

Maison Prouvé

Nancy, France, 1954

Jean Prouvé

The house
in the snow.

Left
Jean Prouvé
in the cockpit
of his glider
in the Thirties.

One fine summer's day in the year 1954, a little family group set about building a house on the slopes of a steep hill. The materials were unloaded from a van and a Jeep. People shouted instructions to each other and climbed onto the scaffolding. Notebooks full of carefully drawn sketches were consulted. Neither time nor effort was spared. Building started in June, in September they were moving in. Building-sites organised by heads of families tired of administrative delay and loathe to live in shared blocks were a common enough sight at this time of post-war reconstruction. This little scene would have been merely banal but for the fact that the man building his family house on this steep slope on the edge of Nancy was none other than Jean Prouvé, inventor and builder, a revered figure for progressive architects.

The son of Victor Prouvé, one of the leading figures in Art Nouveau in the Nancy school, Jean Prouvé started out as an 'artist-metalworker,' although he himself refused this description, considering it tautological. He mockingly entitled himself 'metal twister'. At the end of the 1920s he went to Paris, where he met

important modern architects such as Le Corbusier, Jeanneret, Herbé and Mallet-Stevens. He became one of the founder members of the UAM, the Union of Modern Artists. From his workshops in Nancy came doors, railings, lift cages, all kinds of iron–and metal–work, the fruit of his collaboration with the best architects of the time. Gradually, Prouvé's work led him to deal with questions of a purely architectural kind. His encounter with the architects Beaudoin and Lods proved decisive. From the Club House at the Roland Garros Aéroclub at Buc to the Maison du Peuple in Clichy, built with Beaudoin and Lods, from his prototypes of industrially-fabricated housing to his façades for the CNIT at La Défense or the Nobel Tower, Prouvé's involvement in architecture gradually increased. The 'metal twister' became an architect. After the war and a brief involvement in local politics – he was elected Mayor of Nancy in 1945 but resigned – he set up his cooperative workshops in Maxéville. It was there, in the hectic and confused period of post-war reconstruction, that he argued for a focused (that is, project-specific) form of industrialisation instead of the generalised industrialisation that tended to replace human skill and intelligence by machines. What Prouvé was defending was a notion of human inventiveness that was lost in the heavily mechanised construction industry with its cranes, girders and concrete blocks.

Prouvé's methods of 'intelligently' industrialising architectural components attracted the attention of the aluminium industry, which perceived in it a major new outlet. The misunderstanding was fatal for the Maxéville workshops. Prouvé's new partners expected him to turn out 'forms' and a 'style', and failed to understand the creative working methods of the business. Forced to reduce his workforce, Prouvé, bruised by the experience and loyal to his colleagues, left the business, furious with the narrow-minded men who had wrecked such a fine project. No doubt he built the house in Nancy partly as an outlet for his energy.

In May 1954, he acquired for a song a piece of land on a steep slope, supposedly impossible to build on. He had saved a few components from his workshops: a scaffolding tower and some aluminium panels. Erected in no time at all, the house illustrates in its simplicity and clarity what Prouvé meant by an 'intelligent' alliance between industry and know-how. Apart from its frame and the metal façade plates with portholes, one looks in vain for any trace of hi-tech. The forms and details are all necessary, and the technical gadgets exist only to solve simple domestic problems: sliding doors that open at the lightest touch, doors attached to the concrete by metal hinge-plates, a wide panel of glass in a simple aluminium mounts. The house was designed explicitly to meet the needs of a family: provision for communal living did not exclude private rooms for each of the inhabitants ("and there were lots of us", said Prouvé). Wooden partitions, a rather grand fireplace in the rustic Nancy tradition, a suite of family chairs whose supreme elegance would not be widely

The dining room
with its folded-steel
chairs designed
and made by Prouvé.

Above left
The drawing room
with its fireplace
in the traditional Nancy
style and furniture
designed by Prouvé.
Below left
The south façade
where windows
alternate with
aluminium panels
pierced with portholes.

The house
in summer.

Right
Detail of the aluminium
panels on the façade.

recognised for several decades (today originals are greatly sought after by collectors) all recalled more frugal times when architecture presented a modest face, that of democracy.

Deprived of his workshops, Prouvé nevertheless played a valuable role: in 1956 he worked with Abbé Pierre to build houses for the homeless. Designed and assembled in six weeks, easy to transport, and cheap to produce in bulk, the 'Better Days' house were refused a licence by the French authorities. After this, Prouvé devoted his talents to various causes, sharing his knowledge with architects of every kind. In 1971, leading the jury evaluating tenders for constructing the Beaubourg centre in Paris *(Centre Pompidou)*, it was Prouvé who persuaded President Pompidou to give the project to Renzo Piano and Richard Rogers. He proved a brilliant teacher at the CNAM *(Centre National des Arts et Métiers)*, and was consultant engineer for some of the most remarkable buildings of the age, the CNIT and the Unesco offices in Rue Miollis, Paris. Despite being elected to the *Académie d'Architecture*, he was debarred by corporatism from exercising the profession of architect, and "became involved in a form of activity [as consultant] of which he increasingly disapproved". This great humanist, the hero of late 20th-century architects, modestly concluded: "Yet I did my best".

Villa Bianchi

Tavole, Ticino, Switzerland,
1972-1973

Mario Botta

Left
A medieval
watchtower
overlooking the lake.

Site plan,
with axonometric
drawing of the house.

Between the Po valley and the foothills of the Alps, southern Switzerland sinks gently down to the Italian lakes. Between the perfume of the Borromean islands and the enticing scent of rabbit with polenta, the Swiss canton of Ticino lies on the banks of Lake Maggiore and Lake Lugano. "This branch of the lake of..., which turns south, amid two chains of uninterrupted mountains..."; thus Alessandro Manzoni. Ticino is the land of Renzo and Lucia, *The Betrothed* of his famous novel. Closer to Milan than to Zurich, Ticino has managed to draw on two very different cultures to find its own discreet originality. The master of Roman Baroque, Francesco Borromini, was born here, at Bissone.

In the 1970s a small group of architects suddenly focused attention on Ticino. Luigi Snozzi, Tita Carlone, Aurelio Galfetti, Mario Botta and others were exploring the narrow path between orthodox modernism – post-Le Corbusier – and the neo-rational architecture bequeathed to history by Aldo Rossi. The *Tendenza,* as it was called at the time, put Ticino on the map for young architects in the West. At the outset of his career, Mario Botta could offer unique qualifications. Before acquiring an international reputation he had had short but crucial encounters with Le Corbusier,

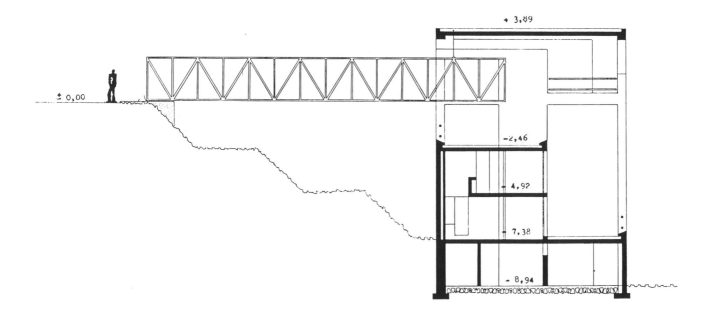

just before Le Corbusier's death, and with Louis Kahn. These two great figures served to remind him, if any reminder were necessary, of the responsibility and commitment, even devotion, required by the noble calling of architect.

Ticino is a small place, where everyone knows everybody else. When Carlo Bianchi and his wife-to-be dreamed of building a home, it was natural enough that they should ask Botta, a colleague and boyhood friend of Carlo's. Botta wanted to leave nothing to chance. He took the two on a journey during which they visited one of Le Corbusier's *Unités d'Habitation* and other modern buildings. On their return, the matter was settled, and Botta could work freely on a project that today stands as a manifesto. The miracle of the house at Riva San Vitale perhaps resides in its perfect ambiguity: it is both absolutely modern and completely familiar. Seen from the opposite shore of the lake, it merges into the leafy slope, like some medieval watchtower or an ornithologist's observatory. Within its grey wall, light glints off a pane of glass in an upside-down, L-shaped opening. The house stands a short distance from the edge of the village, and is approached up a little lane, strewn with pine-needles, which climbs gently amid shady undergrowth. A clearing opens on to the lake, and in it a red wire-mesh gangway leads to the upper level of the square tower. Here we find the main entrance and a workshop-office giving on to a covered terrace. The square stairwell connects the three levels: one storey, with a terrace, for the parents, another, with a study, for the children, the third containing the dining area and the living room with its vertiginously high ceiling and windows running from floor to roof. The vocabulary of the building is Spartan: concrete bricks or breeze-blocks, grey for the external walls, white for the interior, glass windows marked out by their black-painted metal surrounds,

Cross-section showing the gangway and the slope of the land.

Right
Floor plans.

From the drawing room the landscape is cut into a vertical slice.

Following pages
Entrance to the house across the bright red, wire-mesh gangway.

The west façade with its L-shaped opening.

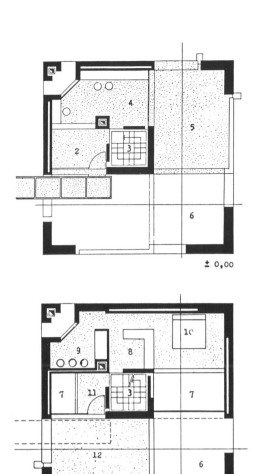

± 0,00

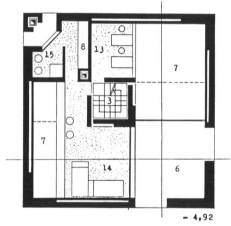

− 2,46

− 4,92

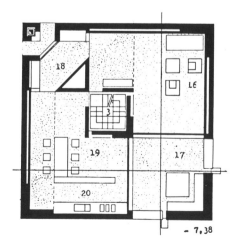

− 7,38

ceilings of untreated concrete to which time has given a silvery tone.

The landscape is filtered and framed with care. A long horizontal opening at the top level and the two vertical shafts at south and east cut out the landscape like a geological cross-section: sky, wooded slope, the line of the road on the opposite shore, lake, near shore, grassy slope, all aligned from top to bottom in almost regular strips.

An architect friend of Botta's was astonished at his talent for sharing the ideas of his clients. It is surely even more remarkable that those clients have preserved the original spirit of the building. The Villa Bianchi at Tavole is exemplary; with its simplicity and its nonchalance, one has the feeling that it has lived a life of serene, undisturbed happiness, without any of the heroic and slightly martyred clamour exuded by some modern houses. After a quarter of a century, the rainwater trough on the roof still leaks, and sacrifices to the household gods in the great fireplace have been few. But these are details. The house has sheltered a calm happiness. The children grew up in it. One proof, if proof were needed, of the house's benevolent influence: Bianchi Junior now attends the *Politecnico* in Milan. He is training to be an architect.

Concrete safety-panels
on the staircase.

The drawing room
seen from the terrace
that extends it.

Right
View in the opposite
direction, onto
the terrace
and the opening
in the west façade.

In Praise of Difference

Monte Carlo
Entertainments.
Archigram, 1972.

At the time when the great masters like Le Corbusier, Wright and Mies van der Rohe were coming to the ends of their lives, leaving behind them orphans of their tutelary shades, consumer society was cooking up its own menu for architecture. The young English sprites who came together to form the Archigram group reinvented the Gothic era in their cartoon-like projects decked out in the colours of Carnaby Street. Inspired by advertising, super-markets and the new conquest of space, their aerial, mobile, ephemeral and consumable architecture reawakened the interest in technology for the architects of the Beatles generation. On the other side of the Atlantic, Robert Venturi, tired of silent, unseeing curtain walls, was exhibiting at the Museum of Modern Art his 'soft manifesto'. Its title was eloquent: *Complexity and Contradiction in Architecture*. Using examples from the history of the discipline, he argued for a rich and inclusive architecture. And he defended popular architecture, that of motorways and service stations, of Las Vegas with its neon and billboards, its vulgar and various vitality.

Archigram was the instigator of a new English architecture of refined engineering and the originator of the hi-tech movement. Venturi can be considered the father of postmodernism and of a historicism that often slips into pastiche, but which had its moment of glory in the 1980s. Beyond their wide (but short-lived) influence, these movements restored to architects an awareness and lucidity they had lost. At a time when the great ideologies and universalising theories were declining, architec-ture found new and vital forces in plurality. The houses designed at the end of this century say as much about the personalities of their occupants as about those of their authors. They mould themselves to the features of a site, adapting themselves to a particular culture and climate. They make use of the full range of technological and material resources, both new and traditional. The globalisation of communication and trade has as its para-doxical corollary the calm affirmation of particular identities.

Eagle's Rock

Crowborough, England, 1981-1983

Ian Ritchie

A tall metal structure emerges from the dense vegetation.

Bang in the middle of the Seventies, a decade already buzzing with all kinds of generous utopian ideas, two young British associates, influenced by the Archigram group and by Cedric Price, decided to take to the road. Martin Francis was a marine engineer, Ian Ritchie an architect playing truant from the Norman Foster agency. And they were not heading for Nepal. By a stroke of luck Martin's mother-in-law, Ursula Colahan, owned a villa on the Italian Riviera and had just decided to tidy it up and give it a fresh coat of paint. The two innocents, imagining they could mix business and pleasure, offered to do this modest task for a price lower than that proposed by local companies. To their horror, they got there to find a house with forty rooms protected from the sun by eighty shutters. Making the best of it, they stayed for six months, on a long and arduous holiday. Some time later, Ursula, who led the life of a globe-trotter in search of rare orchids, grew sad and homesick. She came back to England and started looking for a house to buy in the country south of London. No such luck.

So she decided to build one. And to whom did she confide this task? To Ian Ritchie, whose diligent work and skill with a paintbrush she had come to appreciate. Together they found a plot of land strewn with rubble and submerged beneath ancient shrubbery. On it stood a little bungalow evidently on its last legs. Had Ritchie mentioned the figure of an eagle while they were dreaming up the project? Ursula, who had searched the local records, discovered that, because of its shape, the rock that overhung the site had once been known as 'Eagle's Rock' – and that witches had been burned there... Now the house had its name, and its metaphor.

Ian Ritchie had no trouble persuading Ursula, a spirited woman who had led an adventurous life, to build a thoroughly modern house. A large steel frame supported an umbrella-like structure under which various objects were placed, each with its own specific function. They were at once immersed in nature and separated from it by sheets of sliding glass. The metaphor of a giant bird took concrete form in the ground plan: a 'head' (the covered entrance and central reception area), two wings – one private, the other for guests – joined at a slant, a body (the kitchen and store-rooms), and a conservatory in place of a tail. The topography of the site, which neither architect nor client wished to disturb, dictated the exact position in which the bird could land (or nest). Ritchie wanted the house to be highly energy-efficient, hence the slatted blinds to keep out the sun, and the solar-heating system with heat pump and recycling; in short, a well-equipped glass house in symbiosis with the natural environment.

The metal frame was scarcely erected when Ursula decided she could wait no longer; she bought a camper van and started living on the site.

Then came first misunderstandings, the first signs that the dream might be turning sour. Having lived in Italy, where walls are thick, Ursula wanted walls. Against his convictions, Ritchie was forced to provide the house with opaque panels alternating with sliding glass ones. The house must be partitioned inside; this was eventually done by a team of young architects from the agency, to whom Ursula denied access to the only tap on the site! There were other crises. A fireplace bought from a catalogue was fitted in the living room. A local plumber replaced the heat pump with unsightly pipes and radiators. Wearied by these conflicts, Ritchie could now see the house only as a dream gone awry. The years went by. Ursula Colohan departed this life. The house was put on the market.

Andy Earl is a photographer and video artist, who has filmed and photographed more or less every British rock star since the 1970s. Some time ago, flicking through a magazine, Andy chanced upon a house that was a little eccentric in its metallic modernity and bucolic setting. Intrigued, he tried to find out more, gathered press cuttings, with the mad hope that one day...

A canopy of narrow metal sheets casts a striped shadow.

Right
Sliding glass doors and opaque panels alternate on the façade. In front, a metal trellis for climbing plants.

The central frame
provides a porch
for the front door
and supports
the two extended wings.

Right
The metal structure
forms part of the eagle
shape.

Following pages
The 'eagle'
metaphor reconciles
the technological artefact
with the natural world.

And now, suddenly, to his astonishment there it was on sale. He rushed down, made an offer on the spot. Then, more drama. The house was featured in a BBC television programme the following week, and the result was to increase the number of would-be purchasers. Higher offers. Andy, short of time, mortgaged his London home in order to be able to sign the contract. Phew!

Today, Andy and his family live happily in the shadow of Eagle's Rock. Margaret took a crash course in horticulture – the garden is a full-time job – and every day discovers new and extra-ordinary species that Ursula (God rest her soul) had planted. The older son, at university, stubbornly refuses to hand over his room, which has the best view on the side of the rock, to one of his sisters. Andy still conscientiously phones Ritchie for his advice every time he has doubts about any building work to be done. There is a question about whether to build an invisible garage in a fold of the land, with an adjoining studio for the boys. The heat pump is still out of action – too complicated, too tire-some to get it going. But Andy dreams seriously of repainting the building in its original colours: red, black and silver. The house at Eagle's Rock is beginning a new life.

Eaton Place

Londres, England, 1981-1982

Zaha M. Hadid

Eaton Place in Belgravia: a building like a slice out of the city.

Prologue

"And Mr Verloc, steady like a rock – a soft kind of rock – marched now along a street which could with every propriety be described as private. In its breadth, emptiness, and extent it had the majesty of inorganic nature, of matter that never dies (...) The polished knockers of the doors gleamed as far as the eye could reach, the clean windows shone with a dark opaque lustre. And all was still."

Conrad's secret agent went, as we know, to 10, Chesham Square, the address the author had given for the Russian Embassy. The meeting at the Embassy was the first step in a process that led to the failed anarchist bombing. Had Verloc taken a few steps further in this part of Mayfair he would have found himself in Eaton Place. But he failed to read the writing on the wall...

Inventory

Early in 1980, a bomb destroyed the Italian Consulate at 38, Eaton Place. This was the end of the 'years of lead' in Italy and

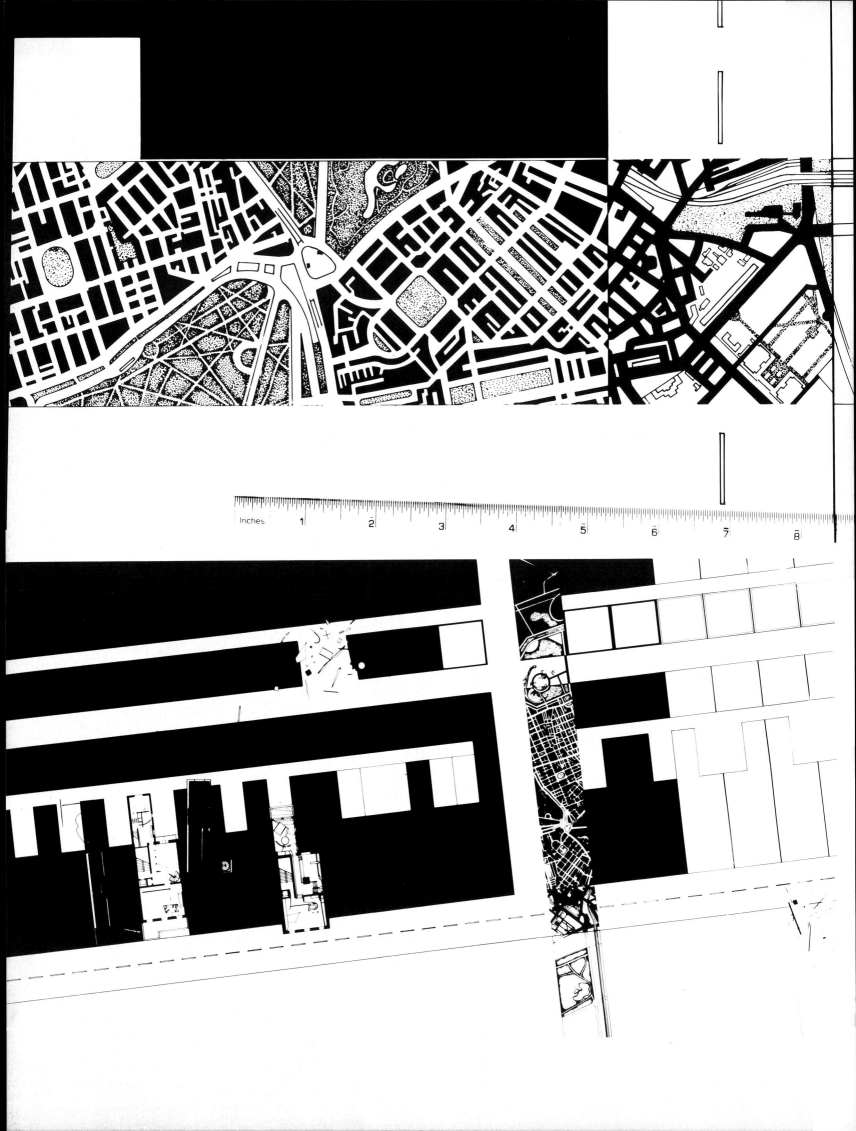

Inches 1 2 3 4 5 6 7 8

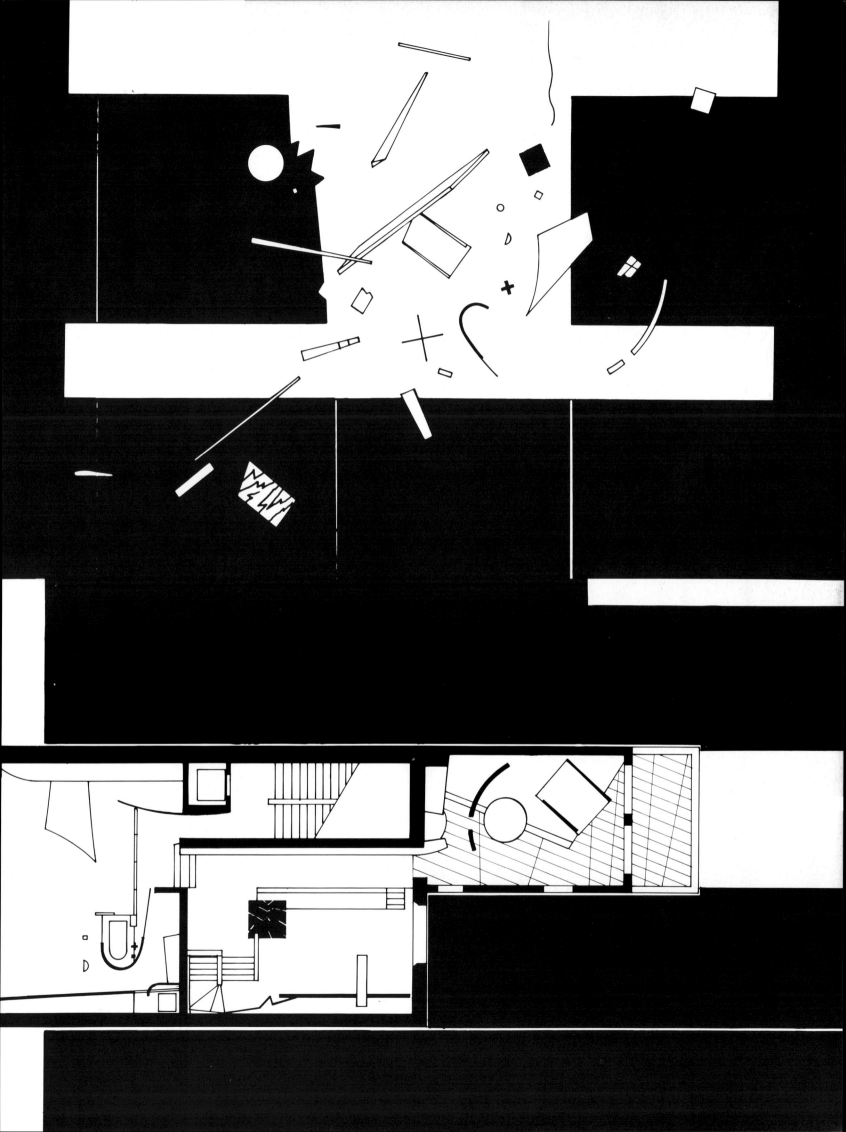

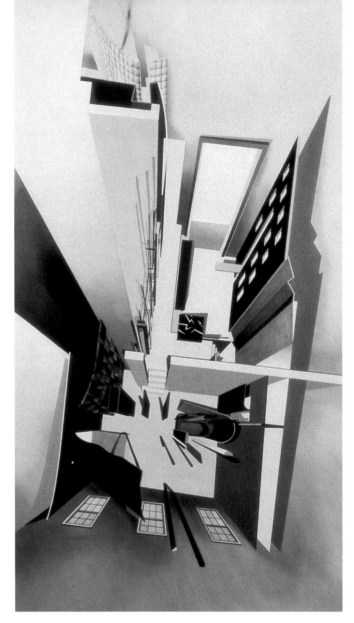

the investigation naturally focused on the Red Brigades, then on the Fenians. It was inconclusive. The explosive was identified through traces of green powder found on the spot: it was X2. The charge was estimated at 16 ounces. It is worth noting that this was sufficient to destroy a town-house, whereas it had only produced superficial damage at the Greenwich Observatory in 1884.

Origins

Zaha M. Hadid had been a brilliant student of mathematics at the American University in Beirut. In 1972, she came to London and registered at the Architectural Association School. Her tutors in her final year were Rem Koolhaas and Elia Zenghelis, who had just formed the OMA brigade on the model of Soviet architects of the revolutionary period. Once she had qualified, Zaha M. Hadid joined the brigade and took part in the plot to extend the Dutch parliament building at The Hague. Was there then an ideological split? The year after, her plan for the Irish Prime Minister's residence was executed solo. In 1981, Zaha M. Hadid was discreetly contacted by a foreign organisation, which gave her the task of refurbishing the flats at 59, Eaton Place. No link with the bombing of the Italian Consulate has been established. The client has never been identified, although the name of Buenaventura Durutti came up several times during interrogations at the time. But this is clearly an error or an anachronism. Buenaventura Durutti, the Spanish anarchist, died in Madrid on 19 November 1936.

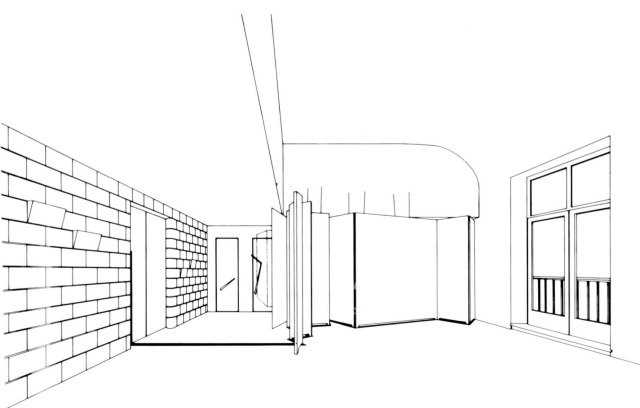

The Building

Having explored Tectoniks for a plan to throw a bridge over the Thames in 1972, Zaha M. Hadid had adopted the slogans of Suprematism and Kasimir Malevich. Z.M.H., "a rocket become a planet", as Koolhaas prophesied, now concentrated on the axonometric drawing that, in Malevich's word, "breaks away from the earth" (the better to observe it?) Explosive dispersion and the dissemination of objects in space constitute a clear strategy: destabilise the construct of architectural thought in order to bestow on it a new and revolutionary power.

At 59, Eaton Place, the plan proposed by the authorities was too simple: elegance and comfort, they said. Its blinding clarity could only arouse suspicions. People would accept that the drawing rooms hosted banal and futile receptions, that the library contained only innocent publications, that the gymnasium was used only for peaceful ends. As to the cloakroom which, with its padded walls, lies at the very heart of the construction, we know that open secrets were exchanged there. But so too was the confidential information underlying the restrained paranoia that prevails in the world of diplomacy and the intelligence services. Moreoever, the plan was circulated only in provisional form. For obvious security reasons, the plans of the basement and cloakroom were never divulged.

Warning: any attempt to link the 'M' of Zaha M. Hadid with figures in Her Majesty's Secret Service will be considered defamatory and legal action will ensue.

Previous pages
Site plan, ground plan,
exploded plan,
floor plan.

Left
Vertical sketch:
a bird's eye view.

Following pages
Perspective plan
with elements floating
as though weightless.

Two perspective
drawings.

Villa E. M.

Tavole, Italy, 1988-1993

Jacques Herzog and Pierre de Meuron

Dry-stone walls
on a strictly orthogonal
concrete frame.

Following pages
The house stands
in splendid isolation
in the Ligurian hills.

"**T**he hill up there's not cultivated now. Only ferns
and bare rock and sterility.
Work's no use there any longer. The summit's scorched
And your breath's the only coolness. It's hard work
Climbing up there: the hermit went up once
And stayed up ever since to regain his strength."

Cesare Pavese: *Landscape 1*
(trans. Margaret Crosland, Penguin 1971, p.50)

It was in a landscape like this, on the borders of Liguria and
Piedmont, that Cesare Pavese long ago lived through the summer's heat, soothing his youthful melancholy. Today, the cars that
drive along the little road that winds up from the sea, zigzags
through hamlets of gabled cottages, and skirts terrace walls
dried out by the sirocco, have foreign number plates. Their rosy-
cheeked, blond-haired drivers come from the north, and without
them this countryside would be deserted. Over time, the pea-
sants have left for Turin, Genoa or San Remo.

This hermit came from the Rhineland. His glance took in the
dry landscape, the terraces of glasshouses clinging to the hillside.

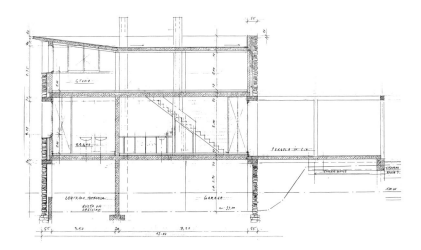

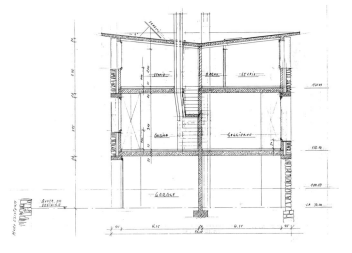

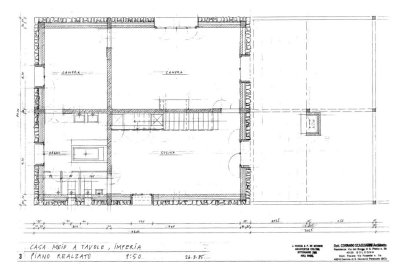

Left
Light sharply filtered
by the metal blinds.

Lateral view.

Cross-section.

Floor plan
of the terrace level.

Upon this promontory barely shaded by a last clump of trees bent by the wind, he decided to build his eyrie. It was to his neighbours, architects from Basel, that he confided his plan.

Jacques Herzog and Pierre de Meuron had been fellow students before working together. By their own account they could have chosen to be biologists, film-makers or simply artists, had not architecture seemed to them the discipline best suited to express the spirit of the times. They practise their craft with an almost religious austerity, tempered by a taste for contemporary art. Sometimes they present themselves as copiers or imitators, which is little more than false modesty or self-deprecating irony. Or perhaps it is a gentle way of underlining the fact that their way of working pays attention to the specific features of a site, involves a painstaking and subtle analysis of the spirit of a place, and that it is this that legitimates their work.

From these Ligurian hills, trailing their ribbons of retaining walls, they took the obsessive presence of dry stone without mortar and applied it to the house like a pigment to make "an open-air painting of the surrounding countryside", an intentional and ambiguous version of *natura pictrix*. It is, perhaps, the exaggerated simplicity of the house's structure and geometry that creates such a strange impression. As if the house did not so much conform to or copy the landscape as suggest mimesis in the senses described by Roger Caillois: disguise, camouflage and intimidation. The house seems to contain all three versions: disguise, in its tendency to suggest something other than what it is (passing itself off as a wall) and camouflage, in its will to dissolve into the natural surroundings. As to intimidation, the sombre quality of its railings and shutters alone would have this effect. But there is also the 'empty, terrifying mask', the bare, sterile pergola on a stone platform more suited to some expiatory sacrifice than to an open-air meal of *pasta e fagioli*. In its harsh, silent presence, its solitude at the hill's summit, the house in Tavole stands like an unsolved enigma.

The stark, ascetic
concrete pergola.

Villa d'All Ava

Saint-Cloud, France, 1984-1991

OMA Rem Koolhaas

Left
An aluminium box
perched on a forest
of metal posts.

Beside the green hill that runs along the Seine (visible from the A13 before it plunges through in a tunnel), there is a district that the century has filled with homes for the wealthy, each one in the style of its time. There are Norman holiday homes, solid millstone pavilions, terraces with neo-classical balusters, gables collapsing under the weight of wisteria, and modern residences straight out of a Jacques Tati film. Behind a bare yellow ochre wall, Italianate in its incipient decrepitude, two boxes of metallic panelling rise up, as if suspended from the branches. Horizontal windows interrupt their surfaces; one of them silver grey, the other a pink, reminiscent of old-fashioned feminine underwear.

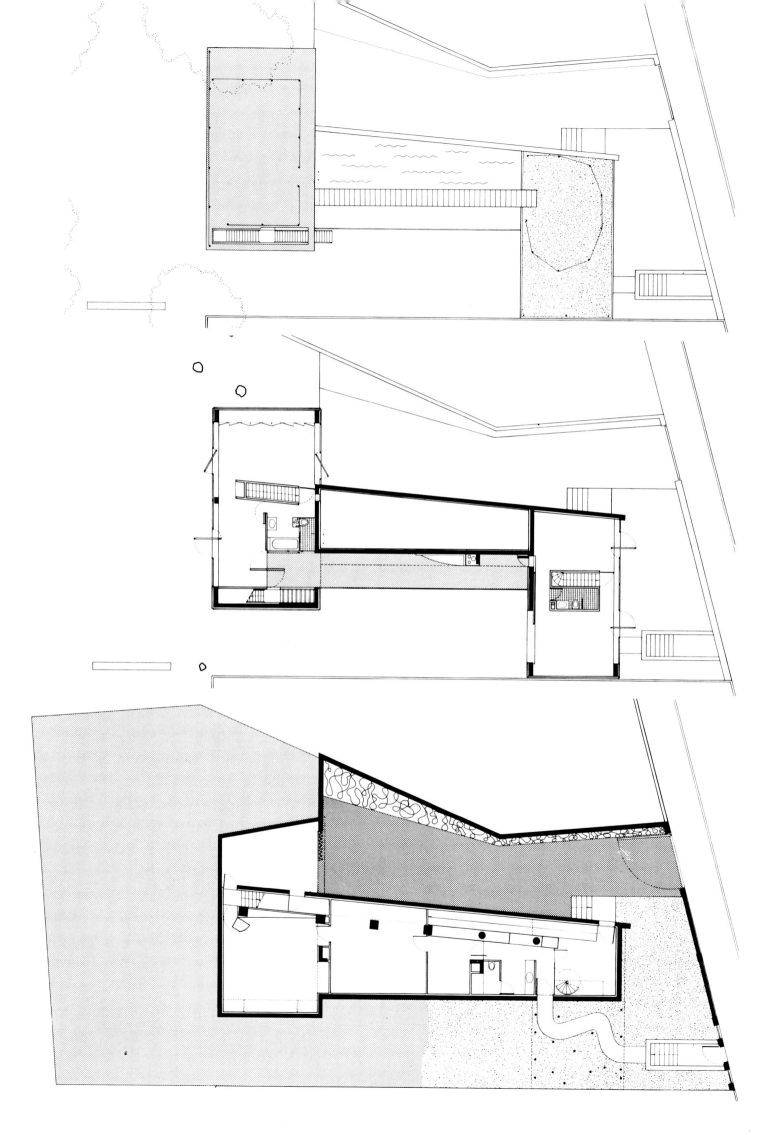

Left
Floor plans. From
the bottom up:
ground floor,
bedrooms, roof terrace
and swimming-pool.

Cross section.

Longitudinal section.

The living level:
an empty space
sandwiched between
the slate revetment
of the base and
a level cantilevered
from narrow supports.

The Villa d'All Ava makes no secret of its modernity. This may have some connection with the veiled opposition to its construction from the neighbours, or with the court cases which delayed its construction. The issue was a trivial one. A clause in the planning laws raised the unfathomable question of transparency: should a pane of etched glass be judged to be: a) transparent, b) translucent, or c) opaque? The client had to go as far as the *Conseil d'État* to resolve the matter and continue his work.

All this demanded obstinacy and deep-rooted conviction. Dominique Boudet's image is one of discretion and modesty. The hazards of life and the hand of fate turned him into a passionate lover of architecture. Over many years he has visited, scrutinised and contemplated the most sublime works of the modern masters: Le Corbusier, Mies van der Rohe, Kahn and Aalto. When he came to construct his own house, he perceived that he was lost without these great heroes. He searched high and low for descendants worthy of them, and he searched in vain. He was on the point of despair when, hey presto! Rem Koolhaas was there.

When he met his future client, Rem Koolhaas had little to show for himself. There were project/manifestos, drawings that were a mixture of Leonidov's Constructivism/Suprematism and old-fashioned comic strips, and one book (which the client had not read). And there were, after all, two buildings under construction:

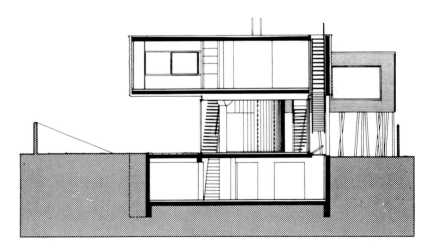

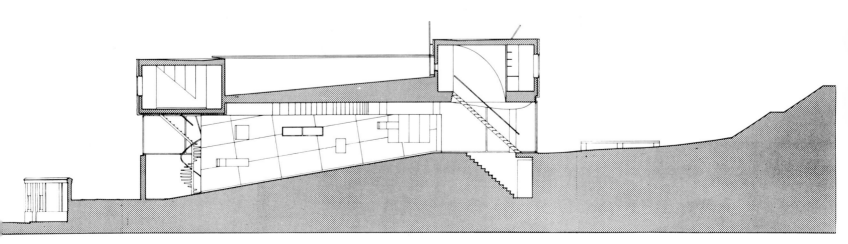

a housing project in Amsterdam North, and a police-station in Almere (a severe building, of necessity). But his approach and his ideas, his priest-like manner, his resemblance to Gary Cooper playing Howard Roark, his imagination, intransigence, seriousness and wit, delighted the Boudets. As did his ambition, which matched theirs. They quickly formed an alliance.

The requirements were simple enough: they wanted a family house for a couple and a little girl who would grow up there. And two other things: they wanted an unspoilt view from the swimming-pool over the trees of the Bois de Boulogne with the Eiffel Tower on the horizon, and they wanted the house to be a masterpiece. The last thing Koolhaas wanted was a standard "house with swimming-pool" project, but he came round to it. As for the other condition, he was willing enough.

Faced with a narrow site and planning regulations requiring that the house be set back from the road, the architect subtly turned these drawbacks to his advantage. The building's footprint is a narrow trapezium, which marks out rather than encloses the main living spaces. A basement half buried in the slope, all slate revetment where it emerges (the vernacular touch), provides an entrance hall at the front, and at the rear shelters a garage and a work-room with a skylight of glass bricks. The swimming-pool is placed atop the main structure and flanked above and below by simple, aluminium-panelled parallelepipeds, one perched on skewed metal posts, the other cantilevered. This configuration opens the living spaces onto three different aspects of the garden through sliding panels alternating the transparency of clear glass and the translucence of etched glass, varied again by shutters of perforated steel and bamboo. This way of resolving a complex problem with stark simplicity lends the house an aerial grace. Everything here stands to reason, and seems to have been assembled effortlessly, with a calculated nonchalance that eliminates any trace of exertion or ostentation. The structure, neither concealed nor revealed, seems inevitably to conceal some virtuoso stroke. It is as though absorbed into the living spaces by the plywood shelving, diverted by the crossed metal posts, or ironically pointed out by the single displaced support that wipes out the angle of the living room (an old trick, and always a happy one). There is also something natural about the use of a limited number of precious or commonplace materials – marble, parquet or lino on the floor, silk curtains and polished plaster – without hierarchy, simply for what they are. The kitchen wall makes the same point: a circle of corrugated polyester resembling Japanese vellum. In its understated theatricality, the house is reminiscent of the work of Mies van der Rohe. But there is nothing of his hieratic immobility about the spaces displayed here. Instead the Villa d'All Ava evokes a kind of voluptuous puritanism (which the client would no doubt deny). But the pleasure and the pride apparent in his glance are eloquent. The architect and his colleagues have fulfilled their brief.

At ground level the villa has a minimal footprint. The upper storeys extend some considerable distance outwards from the concrete supporting wall.

The living area opens on
to the garden via wide,
sliding glass panels
and is shaded from
the sun by shutters
of perforated steel
or bamboo.
The kitchen is closed off
by a crescent
of corrugated polyester.

The corner of the living
room, overlooking
the garden,
is eliminated
by the displacement
of the support.

Right
The villa at night,
with Paris
in the background.

Lazlo Pollok House

Szigetsentmàrton, Hungary, 1993-1994

Imre Makovecz

Left
A wooden façade framed with winged wooden beams like totem poles.

Imre Makovecz is a rare, perhaps unique case. He has practised his art in a country until recently under the yoke of dialectical materialism and nevertheless acquired an international reputation, at least among his fellow architects. The man and his work are, it is true, highly individual. Makovecz's development was strongly marked by the anthroposophic theories of Rudolf Steiner and the shock provoked by his discovery of the Goetheanum at Dornach, "a monstrous elephant that appeared on a hilltop in the morning mist". This led to his espousal of an organic architecture and his penchant for artisanal construction. In Communist Hungary, naturally, the slightest trace of individualism meant danger. The authoritarian regimes propounded for all eternity two architectural styles: Neo-Classicism as an embodiment of power, and 'Heimatstile' as a sign of their closeness to

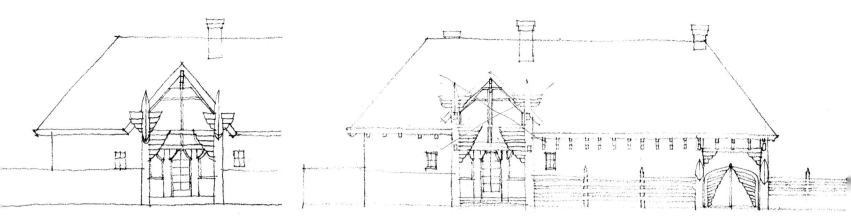

Drawings by Imre
Makovecz: street
frontage, revised street
frontage, courtyard
elevation. L-shaped
ground-floor plan
with drawing room
on the right.

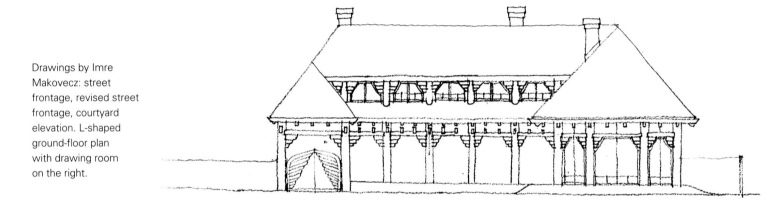

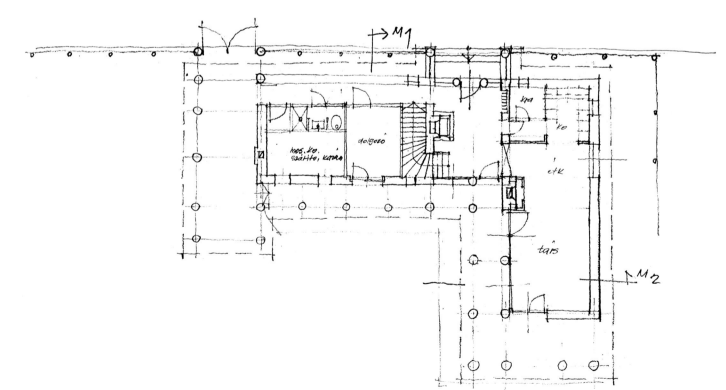

The two roof levels
with columns made
from tree trunks
with winged motifs.

A colonnade of rough-
hewn tree trunks
against a background
of white stucco,
crowned with a roof
of little tiles, all
in perfect harmony.

the people. In a situation where official construction of homes met less than 40% of need, Makovecz, under the cover of producing a so-called vernacular architecture, was able to build not only collective housing and leisure centres, not only chapels and churches, but even individual houses. These houses were built, for the most part, by his clients' own hands. As Makovecz, subsequently observed, their existence testifies to his clients' dogged commitment, their cunning use of lies and trickery in their relations with the authorities, and their plundering of official building sites. In this unusual situation, strange buildings sprang up with arborescent forms, twisted roofs, openings in the shape of eyes, totemic emblems, figures of birds and angels with wings unfurled. In his use of a symbolic architecture infused with spirituality, Makovecz became an ally of Josef Beuys and Rudi Dutschke, who were also influenced by the theosophy of Steiner and adepts of 'thought in action'.

Lazlo Pollok faithfully followed Makovecz in his quest and built many of his designs. So it was naturally to Makovecz that he turned when he decided to build his own house. Situated some distance from Budapest, on a small plot of land separated from a branch of the Danube by a low dyke, the Lazlo Pollok house presents in this modest landscape what is at first sight a traditional building, with its twin-slope red-tiled roof. As one gets nearer, the picture changes: a huge porch with open wing motifs apparently supports an overhang jutting out from the façade. A colonnade of varnished tree trunks decorated with capitals bearing the same winged motif forms a peristyle detached from the white garden façade. It is duplicated in the structure revealed between the windows on the upper storey. The house was, of course, built by Lazlo Pollok himself. The result is a meticulous concern for detail, which matches the architect's concern to invest the building with handwork. In this alliance of the craftsman-like and the symbolic, Makovecz keeps his distance from the modern and postmodern currents of western architecture. He belongs to an expressionist tradition which, from Gaudí to Steiner, from Mendelsohn to Bruce Goff, continually resurfaces in the architecture of this century.

Detail of the copper guttering.

The rather sculptural chimney-piece next to internal roofing.

Right
Upstairs the traditional roof structure with exposed trusses.

House for J. K. and D. H.

London, England, 1994

Future Systems

(Jan Kaplicky – Amanda Levete)

Left
A metal gangway
curves around
a beautiful tree
and leads up
to the façade
of translucent
glass bricks.

The great adventure of the century is the conquest of space. And the audacity and technological prowess displayed by these giant leaps beyond the earth's magnetic pull have certainly had their effects on the minds of architects. The utopianism that has inspired architects attentive to technological progress has found in such leaps an unparalleled stimulus. At the start of the 1970s, a crop of transparent pods and soap bubbles bloomed in the pages of magazines and manifestos: Banham & Dallégret, Haus-Rucker-Co., Coop Himmelblau and others were inventing autonomous habitats that offered the last word in technology and communications. In a half-enclosed universe, freed from work and devoted to the cult of the self, man and woman could rediscover the pleasures of the senses and transcendental meditation. The cosmonaut meets Barbarella. This seam of quaintly hedonistic science-fiction dreams was quickly exhausted.

Future Systems was founded at the end of this decade. Unlike their predecessors, Jan Kaplicky and David Nixon were deadly serious. The basis of their work was not the imagery of space adventure, but the application of space technology to

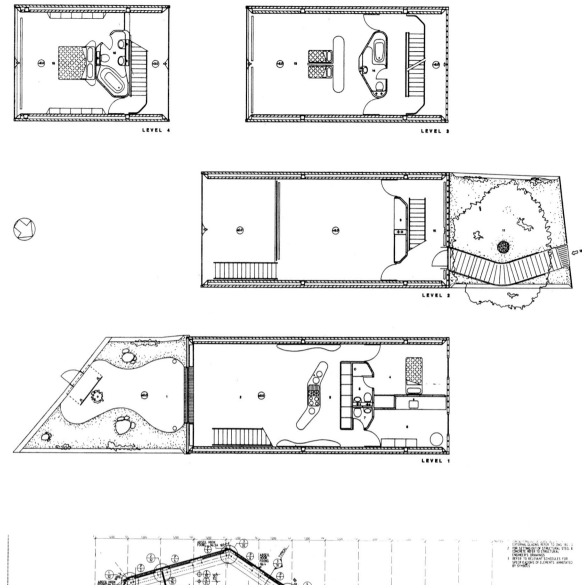

LEVEL 4

LEVEL 3

LEVEL 2

LEVEL 1

Floor plans:
– level 1 is below
the entrance gangway
and on a level
with the patio.
– level 2 comprises
the front door
and access to the
mezzanine drawing
room as well as
to the bedroom levels.
– the children's
bedrooms are
on level 3.
– the master bedrooms
are on level 4.
Cross-section: on the
left, the front façade
and stairwell; on the
right, the sloping glass
façade overlooking
the rear patio.

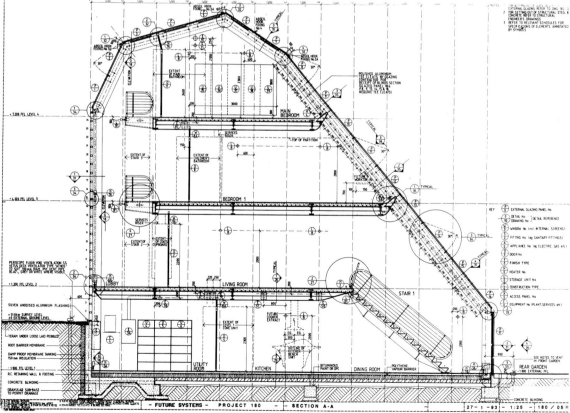

- FUTURE SYSTEMS - PROJECT 180 - SECTION A-A - 27-1-93 - 1:25 - 180/05H

Exterior and interior views of the front door. The door has been cut out from the same sheet of metal as the frame.

Detail of the staircase hand-rail with its steel cables.

construction. To the figures traditionally venerated by architects, such as Isambard Brunel, Joseph Paxton, Buckminster Fuller and Jean Prouvé, Kaplicky and Nixon added David O'Neill, the engineer who NASA had employed for feasibility studies on space colonies. Kaplicky himself became absorbed in developing ideas for capsular habitats. Concrete results were rare. Coming back down to earth, Jan Kaplicky worked for a while in the offices of Norman Foster, who finally had the bright idea of letting him go.

Working today with Amanda Levete, Kaplicky still inveighs against the archaic methods of the construction industry and never lets anyone forget that it is now a quarter of a century since man first walked on the moon. But he has matured; he is now better able to measure the impact on himself of such images of the world as his early education in Eastern Europe denied him. He has kept intact his concern for ecology and energy-saving. And he is as much inspired by 'hi-' as by 'soft-tech'; in his references Stealth bombers combine with sardine tins, and the half-shell structures of modern aeroplanes with those of underwater flora. He has also become more pragmatic and has been exploring the potential of aluminium, that Raphael Soriano first applied to construction in the Sixties.

Situated in the tree-lined residential streets of Islington in London, the house for J.K. and D.H. has been built on a narrow site bordered by a listed pub from the late nineteenth century and a Georgian terrace. The twin, ivy-clad gables, a 'sacrifice' to local colour, confer a discreet presence on what is to this day the most developed version of the metal and glass dwelling. Tall trees give sufficient protection from the sun to a shell made entirely of glass: glass bricks on the façade hide domestic life from the gaze of passers-by, while large panels of transparent

The entrance hall
and the two flights
of stairs serving
the upper levels,
seen from below.

Left
View of the metal
staircase distorted
by the façade
of glass bricks.

Below
The living room opens
onto the courtyard
garden; the mezzanine
staircase is to the left.

A view into the living
room and the kitchen:
the latter is designed
rather as an object
than a room. Above it
is the mezzanine
drawing room.

glass make up the roof and the rear façade, which slopes at an angle of 50°. The primary structure supporting gables and floors is steel. The whole shell rests on a structure of specially extruded anodised aluminium, elliptical in section, and tensioned and connected by cables and pieces of moulded stainless steel. In Kaplicky's opinion, aluminium possesses both the best weight/load-bearing ratio and the greatest freedom of application. He uses it for the somewhat sculptural staircases and balustrades, for revetment, and even for the front door and its frame, which were cut by water jet from the same sheet of metal. The visual coherence sought by the architect has been obtained by minimising the number of materials: white tiled floors, plaster and metal. Only the service blocks with their spruce lacquer coating, placed like flexible, somewhat incongruous objects, disrupt this unity. With its fluid spaces extending into a typically English garden, mechanised amenities – shutters, moving panels, sliding glass doors – and omnipresent, well-filtered light, Future System's house stands as the ultimate model of modern comfort.

View of the mezzanine drawing room.

The master bedroom, facing up at the sky.

Right
View from the patio on to the glass rear façade and living room.

Vieira de Castro House

Vila Nova de Familição, Portugal, 1988-1997

Alvaro Siza Vieira

With a stone parapet and shaded openings cut into the angular geometry of its long, white profile, the house rises from a rocky hillside against a background of pine trees.

Was it because of his splendid isolation on the extreme western edge of Europe? Was Portugal, that land of dark shadows and white walls, too difficult of access for the traveller? The name of Alvaro Siza Vieira was long respected only by a small circle of colleagues. His reputation was spread by pilgrims, who would return from Oporto with the ecstatic gaze and humble, knowing air of the initiate. What did they say, these converts? They told of an extraordinary architect working in solitude on the shores of the Atlantic. Of how, after the 25 April Revolution, his political engagement had taken new form in an attentive dialogue between architect and people. Of how, in this ancient country renewed by democracy, he espoused both the modern tradition and the pragmatic tradition of the vernacular. Of how he was inspired by the light and the colours of his country, and how his buildings possessed a discreet, mysterious beauty.

The rumour spread in architectural circles: Siza was summoned to Berlin where he did his best in the eclectic context of

commissions in West Berlin. He left behind a corner block that he christened '*Bonjour, tristesse*'. Finally, by some strange twist of fate, he was awarded the supreme international award, the Pritzker Prize, known as the 'Nobel of architecture'. And everyone took up their pilgrim's staff to acquire a closer view of the works of this modest hero.

The question of housing had an important place in Siza's work. He patiently devoted himself to the provision of public housing in Oporto, Berlin and the Netherlands. If he also built houses for a wealthier clientele, it was through chance commissions, from colleagues, friends, and his brother. He carefully avoided making this into a field of experiment; in his view, each commission required precisely the kind of work that would meet the wishes of the client.

Not so long ago, Siza met the Vieira de Castros on the beach. A holiday encounter turned over the ensuing years into a deeper friendship. When the couple decided to build a house in the country, it was to Siza that they confided the task. In the hills around the little town of Vila Nova de Familição, an hour to the north of Oporto, there was a plot of land on a slope beneath a pine wood strewn with rocks. Siza erected a platform held by a long stone wall. Preceded by the swimming-pool, the house stretches out against the slope, its long façade looking south, towards the town. In aspect, it presents a complex white mass; its ground floor is overhung by the upper storey, which extends in a fan shape. Each fissure in the walls provides a sheltered terrace for a bedroom. Siza follows in the great tradition of Aalto: each space finds its specific solution, which is freely articulated in an uninterrupted sequence. Here he multiplies long views and zooms, and switches from a close-up of a crevice in the rocks and lichen to a distant view over the landscape by an 180°-pan. It is a virtuoso exercise, mitigated by the studied simplicity of the materials, here employed in all their splendour: the bare, white roughcast, the soft tone of the wooden floors, the stone, the polished granite and marble with their different weights and depths. And the light! Filtered by vertical screens on the long façade, falling from the sky on to the staircase, as if reflected by the hill, at dusk it makes the pine masts ripple over the long white walls. Building commenced in 1988. In 1997, they were sanding the parquet floors. Architecture is a slow art.

Left
From the east, the house has the appearance of a simple parallelepiped with an avant-corps supporting a balcony.

Views from the south façade stretch into the distance, while the windows on the north side provide close-ups of the flora of the rocky slope.

Alvaro Siza has restored – but was it ever lost? – the ancient tradition of architecture as an art of patient research and perfection. In this age of electronic communication, of networks and C.A.D., Siza draws. He makes a sketch, he amends it, he starts again. The drawing helps him to think, to gain a deeper understanding of the project. The process involves reassessments, revisions, sudden leaps of intuition, all in aid of the most appropriate solution. Then Siza will roam around the site, carefully select the materials, and supervise the work with an anxious frown; he always takes account of the workers' skill (or lack of it). The detail is precise and precisely achieved. "Buildings are built", said the great Mies van der Rohe. Architecture is a craft.

Siza has long made it a condition of his art that the inhabitants of a housing or development project take part in its creation. In such discussions he deploys the resources of his modesty, his ability to make people question the bases of their choices, and his persistence in trying to convince others. It is hardly surprising that he has been asked to extend his practice to larger urban developments, an arena full of snares and mysteries. Here, too, starting out from a scrupulous analysis of the context and circumstances of a particular project, he will explore a range of harmonious solutions, in keeping with the scale of an urban landscape. Frustration and disappointment is inherent in this process. It requires humility, and love of one's fellow being. Architecture is a generous business.

Over time, Alvaro Siza has patiently constructed a body of work made up of buildings, exacting in their harmony with their surroundings rural or urban and built with fastidious care. On its own, that would not be so much. But every one of these constructions, be it a house or an apartment block, a church or a museum, represents the unique expression of a very restrained aesthetic derived from the mastery of a rare vocabulary (today it would be called "minimalist"). Walls first flat then gently swelling, light mastered in all its mystery; the juxtaposition of textures and colours in a muted range, dazzling whiteness, these are some of the identifiable elements in a body of work that elicits, more often than most, a *frisson* of admiration. Architecture is a sublime business.

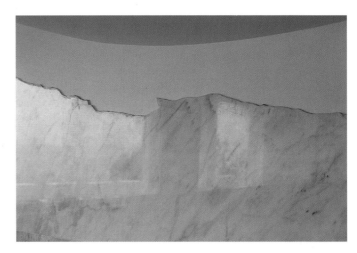

The pink marble fireplace is the focal point for the vast living area.

Right
Views are carefully framed by the window openings.

Following pages
The two displaced masses of the ground and first floors provide balconies and terraces for each bedroom and shady overhangs for the living areas.

Biographies

HORTA, VICTOR
Ghent, Belgium, 1861 - Brussels, 1947
Graduated from the Ghent Academy in 1876, continued his studies at the Académie des Beaux-Arts in Brussels, then spent some time as an apprentice of Balat before beginning his career in Ghent, where he built three houses in 1886. He then returned to work with Balat in order to complete his training. In 1893, the hôtel that he built for the engineer Tassel revealed him as an audacious innovator, transforming the traditional plan, using iron as a structural material for the first time in a private house, and inventing a decorative vocabulary in which the 'whiplash line' became the hallmark. His principal achievement lies in turn-of-the-century: private houses (Van Eetvelde, Aubecq, Solvay), the *Maison du Peuple* for the Workers Party, and two department stores, *L'Innovation* in Brussels and the *Grand Bazar* in Frankfurt. In 1912 he began a teaching career, first as professor at the Académie des Beaux-Arts in Brussels, then as its Director. He travelled in the United States from 1916 to 1919. His last notable work was the Palais des Beaux-Arts in Brussels, a classical, concrete building far removed from the vocabulary of Art Nouveau.

SAUVAGE, HENRI
Rouen, France, 1873 - Paris, 1932
Hostile to the teaching methods of the École des Beaux-Arts in Paris, the young Sauvage nevertheless enjoyed early success in his career thanks to the support of Frantz Jourdain. He built the Maison Majorelle in Nancy, then took part in the 1900 Universal Exhibition in Paris, where he built the Loïe Fuller Pavilion and the Parisian Guignol. After constructing the Samaritaine department store for Jourdain, he became interested in workers' housing projects. In 1912 he invented a form of apartment block with progressively stepped-back terraces or 'gradins': the one he built on the Rue Vavin in Paris, with its white-tiled facade, has earned him a place in history. He returned to this idea in 1925 with the apartments on Rue des Amiraux where his ingenious use of reinforced concrete as a structural material opened up a huge space on the ground floor, into which he slotted a swimming-pool. Until his death in 1932, he was an indefatigable explorer of the possibilities of prefabrication and assembly without mortar.

MACKINTOSH, CHARLES RENNIE
Glasgow, Scotland, 1868 - London, 1928
Educated at the Glasgow School of Art, C. R. Mackintosh embarked early on what was to be a brilliant career. Between the mid-1890s and the eve of the First World War, he produced his most remarkable work: public buildings like the Glasgow School of Art, the Glasgow Herald Building, Queen's Cross Church, a series of tea-rooms for the famous Miss Cranston (a legendary figure in Glasgow), and various private houses. His reputation as a designer of furniture and interiors also led to his being invited to major international exhibitions in Germany and in Austria, where he allied himself with the Secessionists: his influence on Josef Hoffmann or Kolo Moser is clear. From the outbreak of the Great War onwards, he received few commissions. He moved to London, then to Port Vendres where he devoted himself to painting. He died in London of cancer at the age of sixty.

GUIMARD, HECTOR
Lyons, France, 1867 - New York, USA, 1942
After studying in Paris at the École des Arts Décoratifs and then at the École des Beaux-Arts in the studio of Gustave Raulin, a follower of Viollet-le-Duc, Guimard quickly embarked on what was to be a productive career. In his hôtels and villas for the wealthy middle-class of Auteuil in the expanding western suburbs of Paris, he developed an architecture that was both Rationalist (influenced by Viollet-le-Duc) and extravagant to the very limits of the picturesque. Floral themes and sinuous, dynamic lines were a keynote. While working on his most important building, Castel Béranger, he made a trip to Brussels where meetings with Paul Hankar and Victor Horta removed his remaining doubts (Horta claimed that he had copied him) and allowed him to give free rein to his ornamental verve. From the Humbert-de-Romans auditorium to his villas on the Normandy coast, from his Castel Henriette to his own hôtel on the Avenue Mozart in Paris, he created an original style that he modestly christened *style Guimard* and promoted through brochures and postcards. His popularity, which led to commissions for entrances to the Paris Métro, was short-lived. By the start of the First World War, Art Nouveau had lost its prestige. However, Guimard continued to build, now in a more reserved style, returning to Rationalist principles. He experimented with concrete and with new materials like Éternit cement. He returned to anonymity, leaving France in 1938 and dying in New York in 1942.

GAUDÍ I CORNET, ANTONI
Reus, Catalonia, 1852 - Barcelona, Spain, 1926
Gaudí studied architecture, philosophy and aesthetics simultaneously, and gained from this an enduring fascination for the Middle Ages and a commitment to the ideas of the Catalan *Renaixença*. Shortly after qualifying as an architect in 1878, he worked on a project for workers' housing and obtained a commission to build the Casa Vicens. Supported by enlightened patrons like Eusebí Güell and certain religious orders, Gaudí had an extremely active career up until 1914. He built houses and apartments: Casa Vicens (1888), Palau Güell (1889), Casa Calvet (1900), Casa Batlló (1904), Casa Milà (1910), and restored or constructed various religious buildings. Mixing Romanesque, Gothic and Moorish influences, he invented a unique aesthetic, an organic architecture ornamented with grotesque figures and floral and zoomorphic motifs, making him the most extraordinary architect of the century. The great work of his life was the *Temple Expiatori de la Sagrada Família*, which was commissioned in 1883. He devoted himself exclusively to this from 1914 until he was killed by a tram in 1926. His funeral, attended by tens of thousands, was held in his incomplete masterpiece.

RIETVELD, GERRIT
Utrecht, Netherlands, 1888-1964
Rietveld worked as a cabinet-maker before becoming an architect. A pragmatist with an acute sense of geometry, he discovered through Van Doesburg and the members of De Stijl in the Netherlands the elements of an aesthetic to match his temperament. His Red-Blue armchair (1918) swiftly became a fetish object for the movement. The Schröder House, built in 1924, gave programmatic architectural expression to modernism in the Netherlands. From then until his death, his career lay outside the public eye, consisting mostly of housing. Among his most notable later works were the Dutch Pavilion for the Venice Biennale of 1954, a kiosk for the Kroller-Müller Museum, and the Rijksmuseum Van Gogh in Amsterdam which was completed only in 1972, a long time after the death of the architect.

MELNIKOV, KONSTANTIN
Moscow, Russia, 1890-1974
Melnikov had just completed his studies in painting and architecture when the Bolshevik Revolution took place. As a young teacher at the Moscow Vkhutemas, he took part in the upsurge of avant-garde activity but did not belong to any organisation. He soon gained attention for his Makhorka tobacco pavilion at the All-Russia Agricultural and Craft Exhibition in Moscow (1923) and his Sucharev Market (1924). His Soviet Pavilion for the International Exhibition of Decorative Arts in Paris in 1925 consolidated his reputation. Between 1927 and 1929 he built five workers' clubs and his own house in the Arbat, while participating in all the major architectural competitions of the end of the decade. His originality and individualism led to accusations of formalism, and his right to exercise his profession was withdrawn in the mid-Thirties. Apart from a two-year teaching stint at Saratov, he spent his later life painting, living in the life of recluse in his Arbat house.

LE CORBUSIER (Pseudonym of Charles-Edouard Jeanneret)
La Chaux-de-Fonds, Switzerland, 1887 - Cap-Martin, France, 1965
"Man of letters" (as he liked to call himself), painter, sculptor and autodidact, Le Corbusier developed his skills and knowledge through encounters with the most influential architects of the early part of this century: Hoffmann and Garnier, Perret and Behrens. He travelled throughout Europe, visited the Middle East. By the time he moved to Paris in 1917, and founded the review *L'Esprit nouveau* with the painter Ozenfant, he was already absorbed in finding methods for rationalising building, and had set out the principles of a new architecture. A relentless publicist, he also found time during the Twenties to build a series of villas for enlightened patrons: La Roche (1923), Cook (1926), Stein (1927), Savoye (1929). Among his other constructions during this period were a garden-city at Pessac, and two houses at the Weißenhofsiedlung in Stuttgart (1927). In the Thirties he further developed the urban planning programmes that he had begun with his plans for a *Ville Contemporaine* with three million inhabitants, and his *Voisin* scheme for Paris. He created large-scale urban projects for Algiers, Barcelona, São Paulo and Zlín. He also designed buildings for Paris (Salvation

Army Hostel), Moscow (Centrosoyus), Geneva (Clarté building), and Rio de Janeiro (Ministry of Health and Education, with Costa and Niemeyer).
His most important works were completed after the Second World War. His apartment buildings *(Unités d'Habitation)* in Marseilles, Nantes-Rezé, Firminy-Vert, Briey-en-Forêt and Berlin realised his long-standing dream of uniting the best features of collective and private housing. He planned Chandigarh, the new capital of the Indian state of Punjab and built its Governor's Palace, Assembly, High Court and Secretariat. The Purism of the Twenties had given way to an aesthetic whose free forms no longer needed the alibis of rationalisation. The chapel at Ronchamp and the monastery at La Tourette remain the most remarkable examples of this.

CHAREAU, PIERRE
Le Havre, France, 1883 - New York, USA, 1950
After studies at the École des Beaux-Arts before the Great War, Chareau chose to become a furniture designer, convinced that the transformation of housing would begin with interiors. He exhibited at the 1919 Salon d'Automne in Paris and, encouraged by Jourdain, pursued his work in which precious woods and fine metal work were used in sparse, modernist settings. A great collector of art (La Fresnaye, Mondrian and Cubist-period Picasso figured in his collection), he frequented a circle of enlightened patrons. He produced a small number of buildings, including the famous Maison de Verre for Doctor and Annie Dalsace. Regarded on its completion as something of a curiosity, the Maison de Verre made little impact outside a small elite. Long ignored, it was rediscovered by historians and brought back into fashion by the exponents of high-tech, who saw it as a founding statement. Chareau moved to New York, where he lived a semi-reclusive life. The house he built on Long Island for the painter Motherwell did not survive, despite his posthumous fame.

MIES VAN DER ROHE, LUDWIG
Aachen, Germany, 1886 - Chicago, USA, 1969
Son of a mason and stone-carver, Mies van der Rohe trained as a craftsman before going to work with Peter Behrens, who taught him the principles of a neo-classicism inherited from Schinkel. At the beginning of the Twenties he was involved in the Berlin avant-garde and the Expressionist movement, and gained early recognition for his projects for steel and glass apartment blocks on Friedrichstrasse. His Berlin career lasted until 1938. During the Twenties he built brick houses of a rigorously geometric design, and the monument for Karl Liebknecht and Rosa Luxemburg. As President of the Werkbund, he organised the Weißenhof Exhibition in Stuttgart in 1927. His German Pavilion for the International Exhibition in Barcelona in 1929 is the manifesto for the period in which the Tugendhat House in Brno is his most representative domestic work. Moving to the United States in 1938, he was appointed Director of the architecture department of the Illinois Institute of Technology, whose campus he built. Housing projects (Lafayette Park, Lake Shore Drive), administrative centres, offices including the famous Seagram Building in New York, and museums from Houston to Berlin are the landmarks in his very productive career. His watchword was simplicity. "Less is more", said the master, adding: "I am almost nothing".

INVERNIZZI, ANGELO
Marcellise, Italy, 1884 - Marcellise, 1958
Veronese by birth, but Genoese by adoption, Angelo Invernizzi built the first multi-storey car park in Genoa in the Twenties and was acclaimed for the famous clock tower built in collaboration with Marcello Piacentini. He was also a promoter and builder and constructed houses and apartment blocks. At the beginning of the Thirties he returned to the region of his birth and built the Casa Girasole, an extraordinary machine for living, capable of turning a full 360° circle on two beds of rails.

AALTO, ALVAR
Kuortane, Finland, 1898 - Meilahti, 1976
Graduating in 1921 from the Polytechnic in Helsinki, Alvar Aalto opened his first office in 1923, and quickly became one of the most active participants in the revival of architecture in Finland. His sanatorium in Paimio (1928-32) and library in Viipuri (1930-35) brought him international attention. He made the acquaintance of the critic Siegfried Gideon and artists such as Brancusi, Braque, Calder and Léger. Throughout a long and productive career, Aalto built many works in Finland, the United States (Hall of Residence at MIT, 1948), Germany (apartment building in Berlin's Hansaviertel, 1957), France

(Maison Carré, 1958), and Italy (parish community centre near Bologna, 1966-77). The fluid complexity of his plans and his taste for heteroclite but appropriate materials, as well as his social concerns, have made him a respected model for architects of the late 20th century.

MALAPARTE, CURZIO (Pseudonym of Suckert, Curt)
Prato, Italy, 1898 - Rome, 1957
A literary figure and man of all trades, Malaparte produced work in almost every form and genre. As the director of the review *Prospettive*, he explored surrealism, and encountered Joyce, Pound and the young Moravia. As an essayist and polemicist, he wrote on Lenin and the 'Russian soul'; as a playwright, he produced controversial plays (including a version of *Das Kapital*). He was also a war correspondent and described the horrors of war in his novels *Kaputt* and *La Pelle*. Discovered to be the true designer of his own house, which he claimed was a self-portrait, 'una casa come me', he belatedly and unexpectedly earned a place among the great architects of the century.

PROUVÉ, JEAN
Paris, France, 1901-1984
Son of Victor Prouvé, a leading figure in the 'Nancy School', Jean Prouvé abandoned his studies early in order to learn metal work. He opened his first workshop in 1923 and produced gates, lift-cages and railings. The introduction of arc-welding and stainless steel allowed him to obtain increasingly frequent commissions for building work. Prouvé went to Paris where he met Le Corbusier, Mallet-Stevens and the first modernists. He was a founder member of the *Union des Artistes Modernes* in 1930. His encounter with the architects Beaudouin and Lods was decisive: together they produced buildings for the Buc airfield, prototypes of industrially-fabricated houses, and the masterpiece of its day, the Maison du Peuple in Clichy, the first multi-functional work, which combined the market with cultural action. During the Second World War, his Nancy workshop produced urgently-needed equipment: furnaces for low-grade fuels, gas-generators, but also furniture. After the war, Prouvé, now running his own workshops at Maxéville, built housing for the homeless, producing wall-units, doors and facades. His interest in the commercial applications of aluminium led Pechiney to choose Maxéville as a pilot factory, a collaboration which resulted in misunderstandings and failure; the objectives of industrial production proved incompatible with the creative working methods of the workshops. From 1954, Prouvé ran the architecture department of the Compagnie Industrielle de Transport. He taught at the *Centre National des Arts et Métiers* and began a new career as a consultant engineer on many of the major projects of the period. This did not prevent him from continuing his research into industrialised housing, of which the prefabricated units produced for Abbé Pierre in 1956 were a significant example. Until his death, Prouvé, with great modesty, continued to share his skills and talents with many generations of architects. It was not until he led the jury assessing the submissions for designing the *Centre Georges Pompidou* in Paris, and the homage paid to him by leading high-tech architects, that he took the place he deserved in the history of architecture.

BOTTA, MARIO
Mendrisio, Switzerland, 1943
Graduating from the Istituto Universitario di Architettura in Venice in 1969, Mario Botta had two important encounters, with Le Corbusier and with Louis Kahn, that had considerable influence on his first constructions. Along with his colleagues in the *Ticinese School*, such as Snozzi and Galfetti, he developed an original formalistic vocabulary whose archetypal forms are often of rural derivation, allied to a restricted, carefully chosen repertoire of materials: untreated concrete, cement bricks, rigorous and precise metal locks and fittings. His principal buildings – houses in Ticino, a library and a theatre in France, a museum in San Francisco – attest to his maturity and mastery of his art.

RITCHIE, IAN
Hove, United Kingdom, 1947
A graduate of the Polytechnic of Central London (1972), Ian Ritchie belongs to that current in British architecture that combines interest in technological developments with ecological concerns. It is a current whose most productive work has been collaborative. Thus Ritchie has worked with the engineers and architects Ove Arup, Michael Hopkins and Norman Foster. He

was a founder-member of the Chrysalis group (with Mike Davis and Alan Stanton), which focused on developing extensible or inflatable structures. Then, with the late Peter Rice and the naval architect Martin Francis, he set up the RFR group, which was responsible for the glasshouses of the science museum at La Villette and the 'clouds' in the Arche de la Défense. His own office, Ian Ritchie Architects, established in London in 1981, has produced numerous constructions, including the Ecology Hall in the Natural History Museum in London, the experimental glasshouse at Terrasson, and the largest glass building in the world, the Leipzig trade fair hall (with the German company Van Gerkan).

HADID, ZAHA
Baghdad, Iraq, 1950
After studying mathematics in Beirut, Zaha Hadid trained as an architect at the Architectural Association in London. Her tutors there were Rem Koolhaas and Elia Zenghelis and she later joined them in the OMA group during a competition. She had already developed an original style drawing based on Suprematism and the 'planits' of Malevich. She won the competition to design the Hong Kong Peak Club in 1983, a project that was never constructed but which gained her international attention. Since then she has built the Monsoon Restaurant in Sapporo (1990), the on-site fire-station for the Vitra industrial plant near Basel (1993) and a corner building in Berlin (1993). She won competitions to design the Cardiff Opera House (1994) and a projected bridge with housing over the Thames in 1996. She is currently building a housing project in Vienna.

HERZOG & DE MEURON
Jacques Herzog
Pierre de Meuron
Both born in Basel in 1950, Herzog and de Meuron graduated from the Eidgenössische Technische Hochschule in Zurich, where they were students of Aldo Rossi. It was Rossi's reinterpretation of Greek Classicism via Loos and Mies van der Rohe, rather than his historicist concerns, that proved a decisive influence on their subsequent development. Attentive to contemporary art, Herzog and de Meuron found in Remi Zaugg an artist with whom they could work closely. Their works, often forming units of elementary geometric form, are marked by a free and sophisticated use of materials.

KOOLHAAS, REM
Rotterdam, Netherlands, 1944
The grandson of an architect, Koolhaas had a brief career as a copywriter and journalist before becoming a student at the Architectural Association in London in 1968. With his associates, Elia and Zoe Zenghelis and Madelon Vriesendorp, he produced two controversial projects while still a student, one focusing on the Berlin Wall as a monument, the other, entitled *Exodus or the Voluntary Prisoners of Architecture,* on the condition of architecture itself. Funded by a Harkness bursary, he went to the United States, spending time at the universities of Cornell and Columbia and at the Institute for Architecture and Urban Studies. While there he published his manifesto on Manhattanism, Delirious New York. He returned to Europe and founded OMA (Office for Metropolitan Architecture) in London in 1976, later moving it to Rotterdam. Since then his reputation and influence has grown through success in international competitions and some remarkable constructions, including the Ij Plein district and the Byzantium Building in Amsterdam, the Dance Theatre in the Hague, and the Kunsthalle in Rotterdam. He was the architectural director for the Euralille complex, for which he built an ambitious conference centre. A theorist of the city, Koolhaas has tried to decipher signs that might help to make sense of the contemporary metropolis

by studying recent urban developments in cities like Atlanta or Singapore. An audacious, polemical and pragmatic architect, he has made 'suffocating' analysis of a programme into a fictional tool which allows him to go beyond the modernity of which he is a product, and to attempt to reconcile the ideas of Mies van der Rohe and Wallace Harrison.

MAKOVECZ, IMRE
Budapest, Hungary, 1935
Imre Makovecz graduated from the Technical University of Budapest in 1959. In a country where the construction sector was heavily industrialised, he quickly developed an original approach and method inspired by both vernacular building techniques and organic architecture. The theosophical theories of Rudolf Steiner had a major impact on his work; in this sense he is close to Joseph Beuys, whose development he has followed closely. Imbued with naturalism and openly spiritual, his architecture has made an original contribution in Hungary, where a school has formed around him, and has added a new chapter to the history of Expressionism.

FUTURE SYSTEMS
Kaplicky, Jan
Prague, Czechoslovakia, 1937
Graduated from the College of Architecture and Applied Arts in Prague in 1962.
Levette, Amanda
Bridgend, United Kingdom, 1955
Graduated from the Architectural Association in London in 1982.
Emigrating to London in 1969, Jan Kaplicky worked with Denys Lasdun, Piano & Rogers, Spencer & Webster and Foster Associates. He founded Future Systems in 1979, with David Nixon. His partnership with Amanda Levette dates from 1989. She herself had worked with Alsop & Lyall, YRM Architects and Richard Rogers & Partners.
As its name suggests, Future Systems is concerned with new developments in technology in relation to environmental problems. The company draws its inspiration from context and site, organic forms and the human body no less than from the advanced technology of the automobile, shipbuilding and space industries. Using single-shell or half-shell structures, Future Systems has developed a series of projects more reminiscent of inhabited space capsules than traditional dwellings. Their advocacy of an architecture exploiting the latest resources, and their technico-ecological approach is illustrated in a house in Islington, London, completed in 1994.

SIZA VIEIRA, ALVARO
Matosinhos, Portugal, 1933
Alvaro Siza studied at the Architecture Faculty in Oporto, completed his first building in 1954, graduated in 1955 and worked with the architect Fernando Tavora until 1959. His first works, houses and small-scale local developments, bore the imprint of Dutch modernism (J.J. Oud in particular) and of Alvar Aalto; this was linked to a participatory approach in local development. His reputation grew slowly, mostly among his fellow architects. He was invited to Berlin and then to the Netherlands where he built apartments harmonious with the genius loci. One of the great qualities of Siza's architecture is his sensitivity to context and his refusal to sanction the spectacular architecture of the Eighties. In contrast with the latter, Siza's restrained vocabulary, the supple, taut geometry of his buildings, his sense of light, all argue for an architecture that is discreet and sublime. Alvaro Siza's work was rewarded with the Pritzker Prize in 1992. Today he is one of the architects most actively involved in the reconstruction of the Chiado district of Lisbon subsequent to the fire of 1988.

Bibliography

Riegl A., *Le culte moderne des monuments*, Paris, Seuil, 1984.

Choay F., *L'Allégorie du patrimoine*, Paris, Seuil, 1992.

Oostens-Wittamer Y., *Horta, l'hôtel Solvay*, Paris, Diane de Selliers, 1996.

Borsi F., Portoghesi P., *Victor Horta*, Brussels, M. Vokar, 1990.

Bruxelles Art Nouveau, Brussels, Archives d'architecture moderne, 1993.

La Belgique artistique et littéraire. Une anthologie de langue française, 1848-1914, edited and introduced by Paul Aron, Brussels, Complexe, 1997.

Duncan A., *Louis Majorelle*, London, Thames & Hudson, 1991.

Henri Sauvage, Brussels, Archives de l'architecture moderne, 1984.

Brunhammer Y., *Pionniers du xxe siècle*, Paris, Musée des Arts décoratifs, 1971.

Thiébaut P., *Guimard, l'Art Nouveau*, Paris, Découvertes/Gallimard, 1995.

Hector Guimard, New York, Architectural Monographs, Rizzoli International, 1978.

Billcliffe R., *Charles Rennie Mackintosh*, London, John Murray/Cameron & Taylor, 1979.

Costantino M., *Gaudí*, Greenwich (CT), Brompton Books, 1993.

Zerbst R., *Antoni Gaudí*, Cologne, Taschen, 1988.

Hitchcock H. R., Johnson P., *The International Style*, New York, P.W.W. Norton, 1966.

Overy P., Büller L., den Oudsten F., Mulder B., *The Rietveld Schröder House*, Houten (Netherlands), de Haan Houten, 1988.

De Stijl, 1917-1931. Visions of Utopia, New York, Abbeville Press, 1982.

Woolf V., *A Room of One's Own*, London, Hogarth Press, 1929.

Melis P., "L'affaire Melnikov", Milan, *Domus*, No. 650, May 1984.

"Konstantin Melnikov, la maison de l'Arbat", *Architecture d'aujourd'hui*, No. 294, June 1994.

Pallasmaa J., Gozak A., *The Melnikov House*, London, Academy Editions, 1996.

Le Corbusier, *Towards a New Architecture*, London, John Rodker, 1927.

Benton T., *The Villas of Le Corbusier, 1920-1930*, New Haven and London, Yale University Press, 1987.

Le Corbusier, Architect of the Century, London, Arts Council of Great Britain, 1987.

Vellay M., Frampton K., *Pierre Chareau*, Paris, Regard, 1984.

Frampton K., "Maison de Verre", *Perspecta* (New Haven) No. 12, 1969.

Johnson P., *Mies van der Rohe*, New York, Museum of Modern Art, 1978.

Mies van der Rohe, Paris, Centre Georges-Pompidou, 1987.

"Casa Girasole", Milan, *Abitare*, No. 176, July-August 1979.

Nadeau M., *History of Surrealism*, London, Jonathan Cape, 1968.

Alvar Aalto, London, Arthaud/Academy Editions, 1979.

"Aalto Viipuri", Milan, *Abitare*, 1995.

"Alvar Aalto", Paris, *Architecture d'Aujourd'hui* No. 191, Groupe Expansion, 1977.

Tamburi O., *Malaparte à contre-jour*, Paris, Denoël, 1979.

Malaparte C., *Kaputt*, New York, Dutton, 1946.

Malaparte C., *Intelligenzia di Lenin*, Fratelli Traves Editori, 1930.

Talamona M., *La maison de Malaparte*, Paris, Carré, 1995.

Clayssen D., *Jean Prouvé, l'idée constructive*, Paris, Dunod-Bordas, 1983.

Pizzi E., *Mario Botta*, Studio Paperback, Verlag für Architektur, 1991.

Manzoni A., *The Betrothed Lovers,* London and New York, Ward Lock, 1889.

Venturi R., *Complexity and Contradiction in Architecture*, New York, Museum of Modern Art, 1966.

Ritchie L., *(Well) Connected Architecture*, London, Academy Editions, 1994.

"Zaha Hadid", Madrid, El Croquis, 1995.

Conrad J., *The Secret Agent,* London and New York, Methuen, 1907.

Enzensberger H.M., *Der kurze Sommer der Anarchie. Buenaventura Duruttis Leben und Tod,* Frankfurt am Main, Suhrkamp, 1972.

Herzog & de Meuron, Projects & Buildings, 1982-1990, New York, Rizzoli, 1990.

"Herzog & de Meuron", Madrid, El Croquis, 1993.

Pavese, C., *A Mania for Solitude: Selected Poems 1930-1950,* London, Peter Owen, 1969, reprinted as *Cesare Pavese: Selected Poems,* Penguin, Harmondsworth, 1971.

Caillois, R., *The Mask of Medusa*, London, Gollancz, 1964.

Koolhaas R., *Delirious New York. A Retroactive Manifesto for Manhattan,* New York and London, 1978.

Koolhaas R., Mau B., *S, M, L, XL*, Rotterdam, 010 Publishers, 1995.

"OMA Rem Koolhaas, 1992-1996", Madrid, El Croquis, 1996.

Jànos G., *Imre Makovecz,* Budapest, Mundus Kiado, 1996.

Beke L., Entretien avec Imre Makovecz, architecte, Institute of Culture, Budapest, 1981. Translated into French by Jànos Kàldi, Paris, 1982.

Boersma T., *Imre Makovecz, Hoongaars Architect,* Rotterdam, Architectuurinstituut, 1989.

Tisdall C., *Joseph Beuys: Coyote*, Munich, Schirmer/Mosel, 1988.

Future Systems, *For Inspiration Only*, London, Academy Editions, 1996.

Jackson N., *The Modern Steel House*, London, E & FN Spon, 1996.

Von Braun, W., *The Rockets' Red Glare*, Garden City, N.Y., Anchor Press, 1976.

"Alvaro Siza, projets et réalisations, 1970-1980", Paris, Architecture d'aujourd'hui, No. 211, 1980.

"Alvaro Siza, 1958-1994", Madrid, El Croquis, 1994.

"Alvara Siza. Thinking by Means of Drawing", Tokyo, Kenchiku Bunka, No. 607, 1997.

Photo Credits

AD.OB Design Ltd: pp. 2, 18, 20, 21, 24, 25, 34, 36, 37, 38, 39, 40, 41 (top), 43, (below), 44, 45, 46-47, 48, 49, 53 (below), 56 (right), 136, 137, 140, 141, 180, 183, 184, 185, 196, 198, 199, 200, 201, 202-203.
Archigram: pp. 142-143.
Monique Van den Boosche: pp. 144-151.
Baltazar Burckhardt: p. 164.
Cassina: p. 85.
C.C.I. and *les Amis de la Maison de Verre*, copyright: pp. 76-83.
Centraal Museum, Utrecht/Ernst Moritz: pp. 52, 53-54, 55 (below left), 56.
Gitty Darugar: p. 135.
Richard Davies: cover and pp. 186, 189, 190, 191, 192-193, 194, 195.
Copyright: pp. 6-7, 8, 41, 50, 86, 87.
Alvar Aalto Taidesäätiö, Helsinki and AD.OB Design Ltd: pp. 106-117.
Fondation Victor Horta, Brussels: p. 13.
Fondation Le Corbusier: pp. 66-75 (photos AD.OB Design Ltd).
Fondazione Ronchi, Florence and AD.OB Design Ltd: pp. 118-127.
Rolf Frei: p. 161.
Future Systems: p. 188.

Glasgow School of Art: p. 27.
Zaha M. Hadid: pp. 152-159.
Archives IFA: p. 19.
Lidia Invernizzi and AD.OB Design Ltd: pp. 98-105.
Lazlo Lugosi: p. 181.
OMA & Hans Werlemann: pp. 168, 170-179.
Igor Palmin: pp. 58, 59, 60-61, 62, 63, 64, 65.
Claude Philippot - Musée de l'École de Nancy: pp. 22-23.
Prouvé Family Collection, C.C. I. Copyright: pp. 128-133.
Copyright Hôtel Solvay. All rights reserved throughout the world: pp. 12, 14-15, 16, 17.
Margherita Spiluttini: pp. 160, 162-163, 166, 167.
Saul Steinberg: p. 97.
Laurent Sully-Jeaulmes: pp. 10-11.
Suzuki El Croquis: p. 197.
Libor Teply: pp. 84, 89, 90, 91, 92-93, 94-95.
Eric Thorburn, Glasgow Picture Library: pp. 26, 28, 29, 30, 31, 32, 33.
Ullstein: p. 96.
Alo Zanetta: pp. 134, 138-139.

Acknowledgements

This book could not have been produced without the advice, assistance and support of several individuals and institutions.

Our sincere thanks to:
M. and Mme Louis Wittamer-Decamps, Mme Yolande Oostens-Wittmaer, Mme Françoise Aubry curator of the Musée Horta, M. and Mme Luc Vincent and M. Jean Flagey in Brussels; Mme Yvonne Brunhammer in Paris, Mme Christiane Pinoteau in Villemoisson-sur-Orge, Mme Valérie Thomas, curator of the Musée de l'École de Nancy; Ann Ellis in Glasgow, Nina Bernat and Jordina Mas, Casa Battló, and Paco Asensio in Barcelona; Ida van Zÿl, curator of the Centraal Museum, Jaap Oosterhoff, Finette Lemaire in Utrecht; Mme Evelyne Trehin, director of the Fondation Le Corbusier, M. Veyssière-Pommot, curator of historic monuments; Mme Natacha Prihnenko in Paris, Igor Palmin in Moscow; Doctor and Mme Vellay, Dominique and Marc Vellay, M. Jean-Paul Robert, Mme Françoise Fromonot, Mme Armelle Lavalou and *Architecture d'Aujourd'hui* in Paris; Jifi Vanek, director of the Brno museum; Avvocato and Sig.ra Niccolò Rositani in Florence, Lidia Invernizzi, Ushida Shunji and the Renzo Piano Design Workshop in Genoa, Kristian Gullichsen, Marjo Pursiainen, the Alvar Aalto and Artek Foundation in Helsinki; Mme Catherine Prouvé in Paris, M. and Mme Dominique Boudet in Saint-Cloud; Gerle Ianos in Budapest; Sig. and Sig.ra Bianchi and their son in Riva SanVitale; the architects Zaha M. Hadid, Ian and Jocelyne Ritchie, Jan Kaplicky and Amanda Levette, Alvaro Siza Vieira, Jacques Herzog and Pierre De Meuron, Rem Koolhaas, Mario Botta, Imre Makovecz, and Anriet Denis for her attention to detail, relentless perfectionism, and infinite patience.